The Far Western Frontier

The Far Western Frontier

Advisory Editor

RAY A. BILLINGTON

Senior Research Associate
at the Henry E. Huntington Library
and Art Gallery

FOUR YEARS

—IN—

THE ROCKIES;

OR,

THE ADVENTURES OF ISAAC P. ROSE

BY JAMES B. MARSH

ARNO PRESS

A NEW YORK TIMES COMPANY

New York • 1973

Reprint Edition 1973 by Arno Press Inc.

Reprinted from a copy in The State
Historical Society of Wisconsin Library

The Far Western Frontier
ISBN for complete set: 0-405-04955-2
See last pages of this volume for titles.

Manufactured in the United States of America

———————————

Library of Congress Cataloging in Publication Data

Marsh, James B
    Four years in the Rockies.

    (The Far Western frontier)
    Reprint of the 1884 ed.
    1. Rose, Isaac P., 1815-1899. 2. Frontier and
pioneer life--Rocky Mountains. 3. Fur trade--
Rocky Mountains. I. Title. II. Series.
F721.M38 1973   917.8'0092'4 [B]   72-9459
ISBN 0-405-04987-0

FOUR YEARS

—IN—

THE ROCKIES;

OR,

THE ADVENTURES OF ISAAC P. ROSE,

OF SHENANGO TOWNSHIP, LAWRENCE COUNTY, PENNSYLVANIA;

GIVING HIS EXPERIENCE AS A HUNTER AND TRAPPER IN THAT REMOTE REGION, AND CONTAINING NUMEROUS INTEREST-
ING AND THRILLING INCIDENTS CONNECTED WITH HIS CALLING. ALSO INCLUDING HIS SKIRMISHES AND BATTLES WITH THE INDIANS—HIS CAPTURE, ADOPTION AND ESCAPE—BEING ONE OF THE MOST THRILLING NARRATIVES EVER PUBLISHED.

BY JAMES B. MARSH.

1884.
PRINTED BY W. B. THOMAS,
NEW CASTLE, PA.

REPRINTED BY
LONG'S COLLEGE BOOK COMPANY
COLUMBUS 1, OHIO

PREFACE.

Probably no man is better know in Lawrence county than Isaac P. Rose, whose adventures in the Rocky Mountains are here given by Mr. Marsh. Mr. Rose is the oldest school teacher in the county, having taught continuously for 45 winters, without losing a day on account of sickness, and is, at the time of this writing, engaged in teaching his forty-sixth winter's school, and his pupils, some of whom are now well up in years, will surely read with delight an account of his trip and experiences in the Rocky Mountains.

INTRODUCTION.

Being personally acquainted with Mr. Isaac P. Rose, the hero of this narrative, and having had frequent opportunities of conversing with him on the subject of his Rocky Mountain expedition, I have by this means, and also from notes taken by himself, been enabled to lay before my readers one of the most interesting and thrilling adventures it has ever been my lot to record.

Cooper and other novelists have, by the aid of vivid imagination, given us startling accounts of life in the far west, and of the perils and privations endured by the early pioneers; but it requires a great deal of imagination to depict incidents more startling and terrible than those that have actually occurred.

The hunters and trappers of the far west, at the time when the incidents I am about to relate occurred, were a brave, hardy and adventurous set of men, and they had peculiarities in their characters that cannot be found in any other people. From the time they leave civilization they—metaphorically speaking—carry their lives in their hands. An enemy may be concealed in every thicket or looked for behind every rock. They have not only the wild and savage beasts to contend with, but the still more wily and savage Indian, and their life is one continual round of watchfulness and excitement. Their character is a compound of two extremes—recklessness and caution—and isolation from the world makes them at all times self-reliant. In moments of the greatest peril, or under the most trying circumstances, they never lose their presence of mind, but are ready to take advantage of any incident that may occur to benefit themselves or foil their enemies.

Around the camp-fire they are not at all backward in boasting of what they have done and of bragging what they can do.

I was spending a few days at Nacadoches, Texas, in April, 1840, and there formed the acquaintance of half a dozen trappers, who had just come in from the mountains to dispose of their pelts. They had plenty of money, and were having a good time. I would often sit by their camp-fire and listen to their tales of adventures. Some of them related such daring and wonderful stories that I often thought there was too much Munchausen about them, and that a great deal of their talk was extravagant boasting; but a circumstance occurred that proved to me I was mistaken.

One morning three Indians rode into town, each of them mounted on a mustang, and leading another loaded with pelts. They were three of the finest Indians I had ever seen. One of them, especially, was a perfect giant; in fact, he was known at the place as "Big Injun."

"Sam," said I, addressing one of the trappers, "there's three Indians I think would be pretty hard to handle."

"Pooh!" said Sam, "not a bit of it." "See here, Cap," continued he, "I should like to throw down the hull tribe, one arter another, at a dollar ahead. I could make money, you bet. I'd pay ten for every one that throwed me, and as for a fist and skull fight, Lor' bless yer, Cap! I could lick three Injuns every mornin' afore breakfast and only put out enough strength to give me an appetite."

The trapper who had just concluded this speech was a man of about thirty years of age, a little above the medium height, well made, and as active as a wild cat.

I thought this a good opportunity to try if Sam's performance was equal to his boasting.

"See here, Sam," said I, "here's a chance to show

what you can do. I will give you a dollar a head
to throw down these Indians in a fair wrestle,
providing you give me five dollars if either of them
throws you."

"All right, Cap," replied Sam, "give me yer
hand on it; that's as good as three dollars in my
pocket. Them's Comanches, though, and the best
wrestlers on the plains."

The bargain was soon made. The Indians, by
the promise of some liquor, were soon induced to
try their skill with a white man.

Sam threw off his shot-bag, and tightening his
belt, declared himself ready. One of the Indians,
throwing off his blanket, seemed equally anxious
for the encounter.

"Now, Injun," said Sam, "watch yer holt?"

Without answering the Indian walked up to
Sam and placed both arms around him and the
two men took holds, known to wrestlers, as "Indian
hug."

The encounter did not last long. In a few
seconds the Indian was laid on his back. Sam
sprang to his feet and called for number two, who
soon shared the same fate. The third, and most
powerful of the three, threw off his blanket,
slapped himself on the breast, and cried out:

"Now, try Big Injun!" "Me throw white man

sure," continued he, as his muscular arms encircled the form of the trapper; but "Big Injun" soon shared the fate of his companions, as, after a few manœuvers, he came to the ground with a thud that seemed as if it might break every bone in his body.

"Thar," exclaimed Sam, accosting me, "thar's three dollars made slick. Now, Cap, if you'll bring on the hull tribe I'll serve them the same."

This circumstance convinced me that though trappers are fond of boasting of their exploits they are fully able to perform all they profess to do.

As, in the course of this narrative, we may have occasion to describe some of the trappers who were comrades of Mr. Rose, and who took part in many of his adventures, I wish my readers to be fully aware of the character of these men, and that their camp stories are not all idle boasting. A more hardy, fearless, improvident set of men can nowhere else be found.

Mr. Isaac P. Rose differs, in a great many respects, from the ordinary trapper. He is an educated christian gentleman, and, although in describing his adventures he speaks confidently, he does it without boasting and the whole tenor of his conversation on the subject goes to show that he was perfectly self-reliant, and had all confidence in his capability of carrying out whatever he had to do.

THE AUTHOR.

FOUR YEARS IN THE ROCKIES.

CHAPTER I.

IN WHICH WE PREPARE THE READER FOR COMING EVENTS.

In writing a narrative of this description, where the incidents and adventures occur in a region so remote from civilization, and where the characters are so peculiar and uncommon, I think it would not be out of place to give a short description of the manners, habits and customs of the Rocky Mountain trapper.

St. Louis is one of the principal depots in which these fur companies are formed, and the majority of men who join them are old hands, and understand the business; but raw recruits are often taken in, and are compelled for some time to occupy an inferior position—it being their business to watch the camp, cook, skin and dress the game, stretch and dry the pelts, and otherwise make themselves generally useful; while the old hunter and trapper, after attending to his traps, sits by the campfire, smokes his pipe, and makes himself as comfortable as circumstances will allow.

Trappers are divided into three distinct classes. The first and foremost of these is the free trapper. He furnishes his own outfit, traps where he pleases, and sells his pelts to the highest bidder. Some of these men stay in the mountains for years, only making occasional visits to trading-post, or fort. These men often take to themselves wives from among the Indian women, and their children are known as half-breeds. It is a well known fact that an Indian girl generally prefers a white trapper to a chief of her own color—principally on account of her receiving better treatment from her white husband and not being compelled to work as hard as the general Indian squaw.

The free trapper, as a general thing, is very prodigal of his money. He has often been known to spend between two hundred and three hundred dollars at a time in the purchase of bright colored cloth, fancy blankets, beads, ribbons and trinkets for his dusky spouse.

The second on the list also styles himself a free trapper. He receives his outfit, however, from the company, and is compelled to sell them his pelts. He is allowed to trap where he pleases, and never attempts to shirk a debt he owes the company, but is always on hands, (barring accidents), at the proper time, and pays his debt to the uttermost farthing.

The third class are men who belong to the company. These are under a half military rule. They hunt and trap for the company and receive regular wages, averaging from two hundred to five hundred dollars a year.

After a company has been formed in St. Louis, besides other equipments, he is furnished with three horses, or mules—one to ride, the other two to be lead as pack-horses. These companies generally take the overland route to Independence, which place, at the time we are writing, was on the outskirts of civilization.

When they leave Independence to cross the plains they travel in the following order:

A captain—or guide—leads the way, followed by the company leading their pack-horses, and a second officer brings up the rear. Six or eight experienced hands are detailed as hunters. These go and come when they please and generally keep the company well supplied with game.

The guides generally have their camping place selected, the requisites for a camp being wood, water and good pasture. When the company halts for the night the packs and saddles are taken from the animals; they are then hobbled and turned out to feed on the luxriant grass, and the camp-keepers at once proceed to make the fire and cook the evening meal.

At night the horses are all taken inside the ring and tied, and guards are stationed around the camp.

When the company reaches its destination a trading post is at once established. Runners are sent around to let this be known, and the post is soon livened with trappers from all parts, together with Indian chiefs and women, and a lively business is carried on through the summer months.

These fur companies are generally formed into messes, and in the early part of the fall they start for their trapping grounds, there being about four trappers and two camp-keepers to a lodge.

The Blackfeet Indians who infest the eastern slope of the Rocky Mountains are the mortal enemies of the trapper. They are sneaking, thieving and treacherous, and will never attack white men unless they are greatly superior in numbers, and then only at night. They will hover around a camp and will try to steal or stampede the horses or cut off stragglers.

The trapper, as a general thing, has a great contempt for the Indians and considers about three of them to a white man a fair and square fight.

An old trapper, by the name of Joe Lindsey, once related an adventure to me which I think will be considered by my readers a rash and daring affair, although Joe hardly thought it worth narrating. I will give it you in his own words:

"Clark and myself were trapping on a stream running into the Big Horn. Clark had been laid up for several days with rheumatism and I was obliged to attend to all the business. As I was examining my traps early one morning I saw Indian signs, and soon discovered the rascals had walked off with four of our traps. I saw by their trail there were not more than three or four of them, and as we could not replace the traps I determined to follow the thieves and get them back. Telling Clark to do the best he could till my return I shouldered my rifle and started in pursuit. I followed the trail all day, walking about twenty miles, and just at nightfall I reached a small stream skirted with timber. As I crossed it there was just light enough to see that the trail took up the stream towards a hollow in the hills. After walking in that direction about half a mile to my great joy I preceived the glare of a fire, although I could not see the fire itself, and I now felt certain that these were the rascals I was looking for. The night was now very dark, and as I neared their camp I saw they had built their fire behind a large boulder. This enabled me to creep up within a few yards of them. I now discovered they were three in number, two of them lying on the ground near the fire and the third was sitting with his back against a sapling smoking his pipe. A rifle, the only one they seemed to have, was standing against a rock within reach of me, and I at once stepped forward and took possession of it. The Indian who was smoking his pipe stared at me as though I had been a ghost. "See here," said I, cocking my rifle, "hand over them traps right away or it will be worse for you."

A great many of the Blackfeet understand our language and some of them can talk it in a gutteral way.

The Indian who was smoking shook his head and exclaimed:

"No traps—no steal traps."

The two other Indians had by this time risen to a sitting position. Raising my rifle to my shoulder, I drew a bead on the fellow as I exclaimed: "If you don't hand over them traps in one minute you'r a dead Injun!"

The Indian, seeing I meant mischief, spoke to one of his comrades, who, going to the side of the boulder, dragged out my four traps and laid them at my feet.

Giving the fellow a kick in the stomach that doubled him up like a jack-knife, I picked up their gun, and striking it against the boulder, I broke the stock from the barrel, then picking up my traps, I threw them over my shoulder, and shaking my fist at the Indians, started for the camp, which I reached by daylight the next morning.

Some of the old trappers often try to scare green-horns by relating, around the camp-fire, horrible and blood curdling tales. They would get off something like the following:

"Well, youngsters, how do you like the business?" an old trapper would inquire, addressing a couple of green camp-keepers, "but there, I needn't ax ye, fur ye look as happy as owls; but ye put me awfully in mind of two young fellers who trapped with us last season. Poor fellers," he exclaimed, with a heavy sigh, and winking slyly at the other trappers.

"Why do you call them poor fellers?" inquired one of the greenies.

"Well, youngster, I'll tell ye," replied the old trapper, "we was sittin' around the camp-fire, just as we are now, aud I was filling my second pipe, just as I am now, when all ter once I heerd a most onearthly yell, an' half a dozen Injun bullets kim flyin' 'mong us. I grabbed my rifle an' fell flat, pertendin' to be hit. On kim the Injuns, yellin' like fury, I riz up quick, an' let drive at 'em, killin' the foremost. 'Now, boys,' says I, make fur the timber,' an' off I skipped. As soon as I got to a tree I reloaded, an' shot another of the varmints. They didn't like this, an' so they cleared out. When I got back to camp I found two poor fellers killed an' scalped,"—he again winked at his comrades. The trapper would then take the pipe from his mouth, raise his head in a listening attitude, and exclaim in a loud whisper:

"What's that?"

By this time the greenies would be so scared they would either fall flat on the ground or make for cover, amid the roars of laughter from their comrades. If a green hand is sharp and daring, he soon gets over this sort of thing, but if he is soft and scary, he is likely to have a hard time of it.

But we must now turn our attention to our hero, Isaac P. Rose. To do this we will commence another chapter.

CHAPTER II.

IN WHICH MR. ROSE COMMENCES HIS EVENTFUL CAREER.

Mr. Isaac P. Rose was born in Wolf Creek township, Mercer county, near where North Liberty now stands, in the month of February, 1815, and his youth, like that of most young people raised in our thinly settled western counties, was devoted to agricultural pursuits, or, more commonly speaking, he worked on a farm.

Isaac, early in life, began to show that love of adventure that culminated in his expedition to the far West. He was very fond of hunting and fishing, and would spend all his leisure time in these pursuits.

At fifteen years of age he became quite expert with the rifle, and could bring down a squirrel from the top of the highest tree, and to roam his native woods with his rifle, from morning to night, was to him the height of enjoyment.

Isaac certainly did not acquire his love of adventure from reading. He had never read a book in his life, not even Robinson Crusoe. Three months at a district school (this was all the schooling Rose, as a boy, contrived to get,) was not calculated to give him a taste for literature.

Young men who are endowed with a love for adventure, and who are raised near the sea-board, generally contemplate a sea-voyage, "but a life on the ocean wave" had no charms for our hero. He preferred a home on the rolling prairie to "a home on the rolling deep." Instead of casting his eyes aloft to the tall masts and taper spars of a gallant ship, and listening to the whistling and singing of the gale through the shrouds and rigging, he felt more inclined to look up at the branches of the grand old trees, and listen to the whistling and singing of the numerous birds that made the air musical with their melody.

After moving to New Castle he became acquainted with Joe Lewis, and as Joe was a boy after his own heart, they soon became fast friends.

Isaac would often, when sent to the store, sit and listen for hours to the hunting stories told by the old-timers, and his eyes would brighten, and his cheeks glow, as old Jesse DuShane would relate some adventure with a bear or wolf, or how his son Joe shot the big buck, and Isaac sighed, as he thought of the good old times, when the bear, the wolf and the deer roamed the forest, and a hunter could find game worth shooting at.

Thus matters went on until Rose was in his nineteenth year, and many and interesting were the conversations held between Joe Lewis and himself, on their future prospects. Isaac, although the smaller of the two, was the leading spirit, and any proposition that he might make would be seconded by Lewis without hesitation.

"Joe," said Rose one day, as they were seated on a log, as usual, discussing their future, "what's the use of staying around New Castle? If you make a crop in the summer you eat it up during the winter, and in the spring you are no better off. Now, this sort of thing don't suit me. I want to make money. I heard a fellow say the other day in Boyd & Wilson's store that they are paying big prices in Pittsburg for driving team or driving stage. Now, Joe, you know we are both good at handling horses. S'pose we make a break for Pittsburg and try our luck."

To this proposition, Joe, as usual, assented, and tying a change of clothes up in a small bundle, with a light heart and sound constitution, and three dollars in their pockets, they started for the Ohio river.

Here they found a boat bound for Pittsburg, and, as Rose concluded to husband his resources, he made an arrangement with the mate to allow himself and Joe to work their passage to that place.

On arriving in that city they proceeded at once in search of employment, but were not quite as successful as they had anticipated. At the stage offices they were requested to call again, as they were not then in need of help. They were equally unsuccessful in their attempt to get a situation to drive team. After roaming around the city for some time they at last brought up at the wharf, where they found a steamboat loading with goods for St. Louis, and Rose, who was spokesman as usual, asked the mate if he needed hands. On the mate replying in the affirmative, a bargain was soon struck, and Rose and his partner, Joe, were hired as deck hands at fifteen dollars a month, and they at once went to work helping to load the freight. In a few days the goods were all stowed away, the shore planks were hauled on board, and the steamboat, with a puff and a snort, forged out into the stream, and slowly turning, started on her course down the river.

It did not take our two boys long to discover that a berth as a deck-hand on a steamboat was not a sinecure. Scarcely had they turned in at night, and gotten sound asleep, when a rough voice would roar out: "Wood pile! Route out there! Be lively, men!" and our two boys would find themselves hurried on shore to help carry on board several cords of wood. They would again retire to their bunks, and once more get comfortably to sleep, perhaps dreaming of home, when the rough voice would again sound in their ears, "All hands take in freight." At every landing they were awakened to either load or unload portions of their cargo, and this, with an occasional wood pile between, divided their night's rest into small fragments.

In this manner they proceeded down the river, stopping a considerable time at Cincinnati and Louisville, and in about two weeks after they left Pittsburg they reached their destination, St. Louis. Here they settled up with the clerk, received their wages, and went on shore, having come to the conclusion that running on board a steamboat as deck hands wasn't their forte.

After roaming around the city for some time they at last found employment in a livery stable, owned by a man named Collins. Rose was engaged as hack driver and Lewis was engaged in the stable tending the horses. Here they became acquainted with a number of "Rocky Mountain Boys," as they were called, who kept their horses and mules in a stable close by. These men told such wonderful tales of their mountain life, their fights with the grizzlies, and adventures while hunting the buffalo, elk and deer, and their skirmishes with the Indians,

that Rose and his companion, Lewis, were fascin-
ated with the description and informed the trappers
that if they could get the chance they would join
their company and try their luck in the mountains.
One of the trappers told him now was just the
time, that a Yankee by the name of Wyeth was
forming a company to start for Independence right
away.

Mr. Collins, when he heard of their intention,
tried to dissuade them from it, and Mrs. Collins
who had been very kind to Rose, was very much
opposed to their starting on what she called a
"foolhardy adventure." She told them that one-
half of the men that started for the mountains
never came back; that they were either devoured
by wild beasts, or scalped by the Indians, and if
they started she never expected to set eyes on them
again. But Isaac was not to be persuaded; whenever he made up his mind to do a thing he did it
if within the bounds of possibility, and he had now
fully determined to join Mr. Wyeth's brigade if he
could get the chance, and accordingly the next
morning, in company with Lewis, he paid a visit
to Wyeth's headquarters. This gentleman, on ascertaining their business, hesitated a little at first.

"You are both young," said he, "and perhaps do
not know the dangers you will have to encounter,

You may be devoured by grizzlies or scalped by the Indians."

"We have heard all about it," replied Rose, "and are willing to run the risk. The Injun that gets our scalps will have to fight for 'em you can bet on that."

After some further conversation our two New Castle boys signed articles of agreement to serve in his company fifteen months, for which they were to receive two hundred and fifty dollars, and in a few days the company embarked on board a boat bound for Independence.

The boys had a jolly time on board the boat, and were soon steaming up the Missouri river. A man nicknamed "Nosey" had charge of the provisions, and served up their rations. Rose, who had his wits about him, and was always on the qui vive, noticed that the best of the provisions were never served out to the men, and Lewis, one of the trappers and himself, determined to watch Mr. Nosey; and the next night they caught him in the act of selling their crackers, ham and coffee to the deck passengers. When the company heard of this the pilot was ordered to run the boat in close to the bank, a board was thrust out and Nosey was compelled to "walk the plank." On reaching the end the plank was tilted, and Nosey contrived to scramble ashore. The spot was called "Nosey's Landing" for years after.

In due time the company reached Independence, and then commenced the business of buying up horses and mules for the journey. The farmers, for hundreds of miles around, knowing Independence to be a good market at this time of the year, brought there animals there for sale, and in a short time Wyeth had purchased as many horses and mules as he wanted. While this was going on the trappers were amusing themselves drinking, singing, wrestling, gambling, and shooting at a mark, at which some of them were very expert. Rose, who had considered himself an excellent shot with the rifle, he having won a turkey the Christmas before, at a shooting match in New Castle, beating Joe DuShane, who was supposed to be the best shot in the county, now began to think he was nowhere. He determined, however, if practice would do it, to become the best shot in the company.

There was one thing in connection with Mr. Wyeth's brigade we must not forget to mention. The first missionaries that ever went to the Rocky Mountains started with his company. Their names were Messrs. Shepherd and Lee.

The goods having arrived, and everything made

ready for a start, the pack-horses were loaded, the caravan was formed, a bushway or captain taking the lead, and a second bushway bringing up the rear, and the company, with an outfit worth one hundred thousand dollars, bid adieu to civilization and started for the plains.

CHAPTER III.

INITIATED INTO THE MYSTERIES OF CAMP LIFE.

Mr. Rose had now fairly started on his expedition, and it would be difficult to describe his feelings as he saw before him the almost boundless plains of the west. He fancied that he had severed the bonds that united him to friends and home when he boarded the steamboat, Leonidas, on his way to Pittsburg, and this feeling became stronger as he passed Beaver Point on his trip down the river to St. Louis, leaving behind him the last of the old familiar land marks; but the feeling of isolation was redoubled when he found he had left behind him all signs of civilization. In a vast expanse before him not a human habitation or a human being, outside of his own company, could be seen, and for a while he felt sad at the thought of being so far removed from the busy haunts of men.

Mr. Wyeth's company consisted of sixty men, and nearly two hundred horses and mules, most of them heavily loaded with goods for the Rocky Mountain market. Rose, and his friend Lewis, soon became great friends with the company. Joe was a tall, athletic, daring, reckless fellow. Many of our readers were acquainted with his father, old Andy Lewis, the tavern keeper. He was a powerful built man; but his son, Joe, was taller and more athletic than his father. The boys while seated around the camp fire at night would pass the time in relating stories of their adventures. There was one man in the company whose melancholy face often brought down on him the good natured jokes and railery of his companions; but nothing would ever induce him to smile. His mind seemed to be continuously occupied with the old refrain, "The girl I left behind me." One evening, as the jokes as usual were flying around the camp fire, Howell, for that was the melancholy man's name, addressed his companions as follows:

"Well, boys, I suppose you think it's strange that I should always be gloomy; but I have good reasons for being so. I believe I am to-day the most unlucky man in the world. Listen and you can judge for yourselves. I was engaged to be married to one of the nicest girls in St. Louis, and

she was just as good as she was good looking. She
was a seamstress, and supported herself and her
aged mother by sewing for a clothing store. We
were engaged early last spring and were to be married in the fall, and in the meantime I was to save
up money enough to buy a wagon and team and go
to hauling. Well, boys, I shipped on board a
steamboat as deck-hand at thirty dollars a month.
and I afterwards became fireman, for which I received forty dollars a month. I was very saving
and by the middle of September had two hundred
dollars with which I started for St. Louis. Near
Memphis our boat blew up. There were a great
many killed and scalded. I was knocked over-
board and picked up in an insensible condition.
When I came to I found myself in bed. My money
was gone, and I never heard of it again, and I went
back to St. Louis poorer than when I left. My girl
received me kindly and bade me be of good cheer;
but our wedding was postponed till spring, and I
hired with a tanner, in St. Charles, at twenty-five
dollars a month. I understood the business and
made a good deal by working extra time, and by
February I had a hundred dollars saved, which I
left in the hands of my employer. Well, gentlemen one night the whole concern burned down,
and as there was no insurance, my boss was a

ruined man, and so was I. Having now lost all heart, contrary to the wishes of my girl, I joined Wyeth's company, and here I am."

"Yes," said a man by the name of Smith, "and you may thank me for it."

This man Smith was a daring, lawless, desperate character, who had been condemned to serve a long term in the calaboose at St. Louis. Mr. Wyeth promised the authorities, if they would give up Smith, to take him where they would not hear from him again, and this they agreed to, and Smith became one of Wyeth's company.

When the boat on which the company were embarked reached St. Charles, Howell's heart failed him, and he concluded to return to his girl, and taking his traps with him, stepped ashore on the wharf. Smith told him not to be a lovesick baby, but to act the man and stand up to his agreement. While they were debating the question the boat started. Smith ordered it to stop, but the pilot refused to give the signal. Smith then drew a pistol, and, pointing it at the pilot's head, ordered him to land the boat or he would blow his brains out. The pilot, knowing his man, did as he was ordered. As soon as the boat touched the wharf Smith sprang on shore, seized Howell by the arm and lead him on board, and Smith was always considered by the trappers as a captain or leader from that time forward. As soon as Howell had finished his story a man by the name of Green took from his pocket what appeared to be a piece of hammered-out gold.

"Do you see that, boys?" said he, "that's what started me for the Rockies. That was once an engagement ring. Yes, boys, it's a fact; I was engaged to be married—the gal war as purty as a peach an' as spry as a bird, an' she thought a heap of me, she did; but I, like a darn'd fool, got on a 'bender' for three or four days, an' when she heerd on't she sent me back this ring. Well, boys, I took and hammered it out the way you see it. Wyeth was just gettin' up his company at that time, an' so I jined."

"See here, boys!" exclaimed a trapper by the name of Rube, "you seem to be all in for tellin' what started you to the Rockies. Now what d'ye s'pose started me? Now ye can believe it or not believe it, just as ye please, but, 'honest Injun,' it war a cussed ole mule. Tho' mind ye, thar war a gal in it, too. Yer may talk about yer purty gals, an' yer spry gals; they warn't a patchin' to Selina Perkins. She weighed a hundred and sixty pounds, an' she had a face on her like a full moon. She was a rouser, she was. Wall, we war engaged to be married, an' I war to run her daddy's farm, which war about nine miles from St. Louis. This day afore the weddin' I went into town to buy a critter, an' fell in with some of my ole pards, who war out to the Rockies with me the year afore, in Bill Subbett's company. Wall, we took a drink or two together, an' I began to feel like takin' another trip, but I couldn't see how the thing was to be did. Thar war the gal, an' the weddin' war to come off the next night, so I thought I'd take a night to consider on it."

"The next mornin' I bought a mule I had been lookin' at the day before, and arter runnin' around with the boys all day, towards night I started for hum, an' would you believe it, I hadn't made up my mind whether to marry or start for the Rockies. The company would be off the next mornin', an' as I rid along on the mule I kept a studyin', but couldn't come to no conclusion. About eight miles from St. Louis the roads forked—one road led to my gals an' t'other led to town. Just afore I reached the forks a happy idea struck me. 'By thunder,' says I, 'I'll leave it ter the mule. If she takes the right hand road, it's marry; if she takes the left, it's the Rockies.' So I dropped the bridle onter her neck, stuck my hands into my pockets, and said 'go it, Bets'—that war her name. Wall, boys, she took the left, an' here I am. I writ a letter to Selina, telling her to hold out faithful fur two years. I'd be on then with pockets full of dollars, an' we'd hitch sure an' certain, without fail."

Word was now given to bring in the horses, each man bringing in the ones under his care. After securing them the guard was stationed around the camp, and in a few minutes all but the watchers were sleeping soundly.

After leaving the Kansas river, the company took up the Republican Fork of the Blue, and from there to the Big Platte, and here the company saw some hard times. Their provisions had nearly given out, there was no game to be had, not a tree or bush of any description. The grass, however, was abundant, and their horses fared well; but the company was compelled to subsist for several days on boiled rice and bacon rind, this being the only provision left. But there was a good time coming, and although they did not exactly strike a land "flowing with milk and honey," they came across a large herd of buffalo, and that night the company fared sumptuously on buffalo steak, and from that time forward there was no scarcity of provisions, in fact, so numerous did these animals become, and so tame were they, that they would not move out of

the way for the caravan to pass, and if they did
move a little to one side to make room for them,
they would close up again as soon as the company
would pass through. Game continued plenty until
they reached Green river, the place of their rendezvous.

CHAPTER IV.

IN WHICH BILL SUBLETTE PLAYS WYETH'S COMPANY
A YANKEE TRICK.

It would be almost impossible for pen to describe
the scene that presented itself to Rose and his company, as they traveled over the plains filled—or,
rather we might say packed—with buffalo. For
several days, everywhere, as far as the eye could
reach, nothing but vast herds of these animals
could be seen feeding on the luxuriant grass, and
so tame did they appear to be that they would
scarcely move more than a hundred yards from
the caravan, and on looking back they could see
the animals closing in behind them, so that at all
times they appeared to be hemmed in by millions
of these shaggy, ferocious monsters.

Great care had to be taken not to disturb or
scare them too much, as a stampede would in all
probability prove disastrous to the company. It

was only when they were not quite so thick on the ground that a few young cows were picked out and shot. They were then skinned sufficiently to cut off the choicest parts. The hide and balance of the carcass was then left to the coyotes and wolves. In making for Green river, the place of rendezvous, it was necessary to make a detour, as it was considered impracticable to cross a small range of mountains with their heavily packed horses, and here we shall be compelled to go back a little in our narrative, to account for what followed.

In August of the previous year, when Mr. Nathaniel Wyeth had started on his return to the States, he was accompanied as far as the mouth of the Yellowstone by a booshway, or leader of a fur company, by the name of Milton Sublette, and had engaged with that gentleman to furnish him goods the following year, as he believed he could do cheaper than the St. Louis Company, who purchased their goods in St. Louis, at a great advance on Boston prices; but Milton Sublette fell in with his brother, the Captain, at the mouth of the Yellowstone, with a keel-boat loaded with merchandise, and while Wyeth pursued his way eastward to purchase the Indian goods which were intended to supply the wants of the fur trader in the Rocky mountains, at a profit to himself and an advantage to them, the captain was persuading his brother not to encourage any interloper in the Indian trade, but to continue to buy goods from himself, as formerly. So potent were his arguments that Milton yielded to them, in spite of his engagement to Wyeth.

When Captain Bill Sublette found that Wyeth had started with his company for the Rocky mountains, he gathered his party together and followed, with a large supply of goods, and contrived to arrive at the turning off place a few hours after Wyeth's company had left. Instead of following after them, he led his party across the mountains by a path known only to himself, and reached the rendezvous several days in advance. Here he found the fur companies, trappers and Indians waiting for their supplies. Trade was at once commenced, and when Wyeth arrived, Bill Sublette had disposed of his goods and gathered in all the skins in the market. This path is called "Sublette's cut off" to this day.

When Rose and his company, after their long detour, again struck the track leading to the rendezvous they were much surprised, and not a little scared, at seeing a big trail going in that direction. At first they thought it was a large body of Indians, but the initiated among them at once pronounced it to be a white man's trail; but it was not until reaching the rendezvous on the Green river they discovered the trick Bill Sublette played them.

Mr. Wyeth was very much put out when he found that Milton Sublette had gone back on his promise. He was now placed in a very unpleasant predicament. He was there with a company of sixty men, one hundred thousand dollars, and no purchaser. But Wyeth was a yankee, and could not easily be put down. So, after resting a few days, he started on with his company over the mountains for Snake river.

Rose and his friend Lewis had never seen a trading camp before, and were much pleased and amused with the proceedings. There were about five hundred persons there, consisting of the fur companies, free traders, Nez Perces and Flat Head Indians, and many Indian women and children. Some of these women, the wives of the free traders, were showily, and even gaudily dressed. Besides the human beings, there were about two thousand horses and mules, and the whole scene would appear to the eye of a stranger picturesque and fantastic. But we must follow Mr. Rose and his party to the Snake river.

As they crossed the mountains in the fall they had what might be called a good time. Game, as a general thing, was abundant, and they were not molested by Indians. In passing down Lewis' Fork into Jackson's big hole, the trappers were compelled to cross the side of a mountain. The ledge on which they traveled being five hundred feet above the river, and in some places so narrow they were obliged to travel in single file. It was in traversing this path that a circumstance occurred that came near putting an end to the mortal career of Joe Lewis. He was leading a large mule, called Remus, which he had led from Independence, on whose back were two bales of tobacco, each weighing one hundred pounds, the leading rope being fastened to the pummel of Joe's saddle. In one place the path was not more than four or five feet wide. In passing this narrow place, one of the bales of tobacco struck against a rock, knocking the mule over the ledge. Fortunately for Lewis, the leading rope broke, and the mule fell about two hundred feet before it struck the rock, then bounding off, fell three hundred feet into the swollen waters of the river below, and poor old Remus and the tobacco were seen no more.

This was a great loss to Mr. Wyeth, as tobacco was selling at two dollars a pound.

On arriving at Snake river they commenced at once to build a fort. This was a big undertaking, as they had no wagons to haul their timber. Logs were cut and dragged or carried to the spot needed where they were placed in an upright position, side by side, and about three feet in the ground. In this manner a large space was enclosed, and while part of the men were engaged in the outer palisade, others were constructing a log house in the enclosure in which to store the goods. They gave it the name of Fort Hall.

As soon as the fort was built and the goods securely housed, Wyeth thought it high time to commence business, and a party of men were at once sent off, under the command of Joseph Gale, to trap Beaver in the Blackfoot country. Among them was Rose and Joe Lewis.

That portion of the Rocky mountains known as the Blackfoot country lies on the eastern slope, and upon the headwaters and tributaries of the Missouri, a country very productive in furs, and furnishing an abundance of game; but it was also the most dangerous of all the northern fur-hunting territory, as it was the home of those two nations of desperadoes, the Crows and Blackfeet. Desperate encounters and hair-breadth escapes were incidents of daily occurrence to some of the numerous trapping parties, and Rose and his small party, under Gale, were now in a country where they were, at any moment, likely to "see the elephant," or, in other words, Blackfeet or grizzlies were likely to cross their path or pounce upon them from behind any rock or tree. They at length arrived at a small stream running into the Gallatin, and here trapping commenced in dead earnest. Although Rose and Lewis, like all other green-horns, were compelled to be camp-keepers, they contrived to steal enough time for an occasional hunt, and as game was plenty, and Rose a dead shot, they kept their lodge well supplied with fresh provisions. Besides this, he took every opportunity of accompanying the trappers, and soon became an expert in that business.

Rose, on account of his pluck and good humor, had become a great favorite with his companions, and if a trapper sometimes felt like staying in the lodge, he allowed Rose to take his place, to visit, bait, and set his traps, and in a short time Rose was considered as good a trapper as any in the company. Things had gone off smoothly and pleasantly for some time, but, alas, for the mutability of human events, they were soon to look on the dark and horrible side of the picture.

CHAPTER V.

IN WHICH ROSE AND HIS COMPANY ARE ATTACKED BY
BLACKFEET INDIANS.

Rose and his party, after trapping for some time
on the small stream running into the Gallatin,
concluded to move to the headwaters of the Salmon
river.

When they started from Fort Hall they had
taken with them several pack horses, loaded with
goods, with the intention of trading with any of
the friendly Indians or free-trappers they might
come across, and it was with this intention they
broke camp, and started for Salmon river.

About daylight the next morning they started,
and just before noon they saw a herd of buffalo
feeding on the plain. Rose contrived to get near
enough to them to shoot a fat, young cow, and, as
usual, the animal was skinned sufficiently to enable
them to cut off the fleece and hump. This, together
with the tongue, was all they wanted, the balance
of the carcass being left to the wolves. The meat
was tied up in a piece of tent-cloth and placed on
a horse, and at noon they stopped for dinner near
a small stream, along the banks of which was a
thick growth of young willows. The packs and
saddles were taken from the horses and they were

turned loose to feed. The men soon gathered a quantity of dry grass, brush and buffalo chips, and soon had a good fire going. Over this three sticks were placed, so as to form a tripod, on which was hung their camp-kettle. Hump ribs were stood around the fire to roast, and large, juicy buffalo steaks were broiling on the hot coals, emitting a most appetizing aroma.

They were encamped just at the edge of a plain they had just crossed, and were approaching a more hilly part of the country, and just as their steaks were done to a turn, they were startled by hearing the most horrid yells that ever fell on mortal ear. It was the war-whoop of about sixty Blackfeet Indians, mounted and galloping toward them. It is said that a drowning man will catch at a straw, and just as instinctively does a Rocky mountain trapper, in moments of peril, grasp his trusty rifle. It is his companion and his best and truest friend. With a Hawkins rifle in his possession he feels confident and self-reliant, and does not fear to cope with any odds, or encounter any danger. As the horrible, blood-curdling war-cry of the savages fell on their ears, each trapper grasped his rifle and sprang to his feet. The Indians were not more than two hundred yards distant, and coming like the wind.

"To cover, boys!" shouted Mark Head, one of
the trappers, and rushing forward, he dashed into
the thick growth of willows, closely followed by
his companions, amid a shower of bullets and
arrows, but fortunately none of them were hurt.
The place where the willows grew was a swamp,
nearly six inches deep with mud and water. Here
they were compelled to lie on their faces. Each
man selected a heavy bunch of willows, behind
which to secrete himself, and keeping his head
close to the roots so that he could not be seen by
the Indians. Into these bushes the savages poured
shower after shower of arrows and bullets, without
any response from the trappers, they not daring to
shoot lest the smoke from their rifles should betray
their locality, and make them a target for the
arrows of their enemies. In the meantime part of
the Indians took possession of the camp, ripped
open the bales of goods with their hunting-knives
and scattered their contents. One Indian wrapped
around him a red blanket, and picking up about a
dozen more placed them on his horse, with the
intention of carrying them off, when the crack of
a rifle was heard in the bushes, and the Indian
with the red blanket fell to the ground, dead. This
enraged the Indians, and they again made for the
willows, yelling furiously; and pouring in another

volley, returned to the camp and commenced to load the goods. Again the crack of a single rifle was heard in the willows and another Indian bit the dust. This caused them to hurry up their movements. Among the goods were several bales of red cloth. Two of the Indians had taken the ends of it, fastened it around their waists, and when the last shot hurried them off they galloped over the plains, the cloth unrolling as they went, and it looked, on the green sward, like streaks of red fire behind them. As soon as the Indians got out of rifle range they commenced gathering up the trappers' horses.

Rose thought this was a good time to visit the camp, about fifty yards distant, and try and save something. Accordingly, accompanied by Joe Lewis, and a trapper named Nick Gan, they started for the camp, but had scarcely reached it when they were perceived by the Indians, who immediately mounted their horses and dashed towards them. Rose and Lewis, however, picked up a pack containing between thirty and forty traps, with which they contrived to reach the willows before the Indians came up. Gan also got safe to cover with a camp-kettle. Pouring in another volley the Indians commenced gathering up the rest of the goods. These they hurriedly placed on their horses and again started for the plains. The trappers now arose and poured in a volley which knocked over three more of the Indians and wounded several others.

The Blackfeet now gathered in a body, about three hundred yards from the camp, and seemed to be holding a council of war.

"I think," said Gale, the leader of the party, "them cussed redskins have had enough of it."

"Not a bit of it," replied Charles Warfield; (Charlie had fought the Blackfeet before,) "they'll be back, you can bet high on that, and they have not yet given their death howl."

"To cover, boys," shouted Rose, "here they come, and I think they mean business this time," and again the trappers stretched themselves in the mud and water. The savages came on, yelling like demons, and this time actually approached the edge of the willows where the men were concealed, and poured in their arrows in every direction, and gathering up everything that was left about the camp, even the saddles, they wheeled and started for the plains. Again the trappers poured in a volley at the retreating foe, and two more Indians toppled over, while some of the others were badly wounded, and were held on their horses by their companions. As soon as they reached a safe dis-

tance the Indians dismounted and formed themselves into a ring around their dead and wounded,
and now commenced the death howl, or Indian
lament, this being a mixture of groans, shrieks
and yells, all uniting in one horrible discord.
After continuing this at intervals of about fifteen
minutes, they secured their dead and wounded,
together with the goods they had stolen, on their
horses, with a parting yell of rage and defiance,
they departed, leaving the trappers in possession
of their camp. They were now, however, in a bad
situation. Their horses, saddles and goods were
gone, nothing but their rifles and a few traps left,
and the lookout seemed not very promising.

"Boys," said Rose. whose good humor and spirits
nothing seemed to daunt, "there's no use crying
over spilt milk. I see the red cusses have left us
our meat; let's finish our dinner."

This proposition was at once agreed to. The only
thing that appeared to have been left was the meat
and a bag of coffee. This the Indians had ripped
open and scattered on the ground, but the boys
gathered it up as well as they could, and raking
together the fire, they soon had an excellent meal
of buffalo steak and coffee prepared.

"Boys," said Lewis, who was their chief cook,
"things aint just as handy around here as they are

at dad's tavern in New Castle, but let's make our-
selves as comfortable as we can. I'm goin' to have
a redskin seat anyhow," and stepping to one side,
he caught a dead Indian by the heels, dragged the
body toward the fire, and took a seat upon his
carcass, where he remained till he had finished his
meal. A council was now held in which it was
decided to return to the Gallatin river, which they
accordingly did, and two days afterward were
joined by a party of trappers belonging to the
American Fur Company, among whom were Kit
Carson, Joe Meek, Jack Larrison, and others, and
now the adventurous part of their career commenced in good earnest.

CHAPTER VI.

IN WHICH ROSE AND KIT CARSON STARTS ON A PER-
ILOUS JOURNEY.

Bridger and his party found Rose and his companions in rather a deplorable condition. In fact
they were, to use a common expression, "hard up."
Although they had fought and driven off a body
of Indians that outnumbered them three to one,
still the victory was very dearly purchased. The
redskins had taken all their horses and goods,

leaving them nothing but their rifles and a few traps, and they had about made up their minds to return to Fort Hall, when Bridger and his party arrived.

Kit Carson, one of the newcomers, was a young and active trapper, small in stature, brave as a lion and full of reckless daring. He at once formed the acquaintance of our friend Rose. It may have been because they were about of a size—Carson weighing about one hundred and twenty-five pounds and Rose about five pounds heavier, or a congeniality of disposition drew them together, as they became fast friends.

On the second evening after the arrival of the new party about a dozen of Flathead Indians camped near by. These Indians being friendly, Kit Carson and Rose, after they had eaten their suppers, visited the Indian camp to have a talk with them. Their leader appeared to be well known to Carson, and could talk some English. He informed the trappers that his party had been attacked by Blackfeet Indians, who had killed several of their number. Carson addressed the leader as "Jack," and after some little questioning ascertained that the Blackfeet were encamped some twenty-five or thirty miles distant, where they expected to be joined by some more of their tribe, when they would most likely return and attack the trappers. Rose asked Carson if he thought it was the same party who had attacked them a few days before. On being questioned the Indian replied:

"Blackfeet much horse—much blanket—much bead—much knife. Blackfeet steal—Blackfeet are dogs!"

"Hurrah for you!" cried Kit, slapping him on the shoulders. "Can you take us to the Blackfoot camp?" The Indian nodded assent.

"How long will it take us to go there and back?" inquired Carson. The Indian pointed his finger toward the west, where the sun had just set, as he replied, "Sun go—me go!" and pointing his finger toward the east, he continued, "Sun come—me come!"

"That's the talk," said Carson. "He says we can be back by sun-up. I think we can get back some of the horses them red cusses have stole. Anyhow, I'm going to try it. Will you go along? I tell you beforehand it is a ticklish business; but half a dozen good horses are worth a risk."

"All right, Kit," replied Rose, "count me in."

Just then Bridger, a tall, powerful man, came up, and was informed by Carson of their intention to visit the Blackfeet camp.

"All right," said Bridger, "but be careful boys, and keep yer eyes skinned, or ye may lose yer hair."

"Now then, Jack," said Carson, "heave ahead," and the three started on their perilous journey.

The Indian took the lead, closely followed by Carson, Rose bringing up the rear. It was a bright starlight night, and before them extended a plain as far as the eye could reach. After walking some distance Jack broke into a dog trot, gradually increasing his speed as he went on, until he got into what is called a lope, the white men keeping close behind him. This pace was kept up for nearly ten miles, until they reached a small stream. Here they stopped to slake their thirst. Crossing this stream they again started on a run, and after going about five miles they found they were approaching a ridge or spur of a mountain, running far out into the plain. They were now compelled to go at a slower pace. Huge boulders and rocks were scattered around in every direction, and they had some difficulty in crossing the rocky ridge. On the top, however, they again had good walking, and the descent on the other side was not so stony, and on reaching the bottom of the hill they again struck the plain, and their journey was resumed as before. After traveling about eight miles they reached a stream, on the banks of which was a growth of willow and cottonwood. The three men crossed and moved up the stream on the other side, keeping close to the bushes, so that they could not be seen by any one out on the plain. They kept on in this direction for about a mile when the Indian suddenly paused, and laying down, placed his ear to the ground. Carson did the same, and springing quickly to his feet, he exclaimed: "It's all right; they are over yonder." Rose also determined to try the experiment, and placing his ear to the ground he could plainly hear horses stamping at no great distance. The three continued moving slowly up the stream until they reached a position opposite to where the horses were feeding. Some of the animals were not more than a hundred yards distant, and one mule, or pony, which had straggled from the rest, was grazing within ten or a dozen yards of them. Just as our friends were considering what was best to be done, two Indians came galloping towards them. Their business appeared to be to drive in any of the animals that might attempt to stray. One of them rode along the main body of the horses, while the other came toward the spot where the men were concealed, in order, no doubt to drive in the mule. The Indian's horse, scenting danger, refused to approach the bushes. After trying in vain to urge him forward, the Indian dismounted, and leading his horse, approached within a few feet of the bushes where Rose and his party were hid, and stooping forward, he commenced parting the willows with his long spear. Just then Jack, the Flathead Indian, sprang upon him like a wildcat, and with a tremendous blow of his tomahawk laid him dead at his feet; at the same time grasping the bridle, he contrived after a short struggle to secure the Indian's horse. The other Indian being out of sight, Jack mounted the animal he had captured, and riding forward, with Rose and Carson walking on either side of him, they were soon among the drove of horses, where they moved cautiously, so as to not cause a stampede.

Rose now commenced looking around in hopes of discovering his own horse, to which he had become much attached. Seeing one that he thought resembled it, he crept cautiously toward the animal and then recognized it as a beautiful bay mare, belonging to Gale, the leader of the party. A halter was fastened around its neck, which he contrived to seize and at once mounted his prize and started to join his companions. On reaching them he found they had secured four or five horses,

among which was his own, and the one belonging
to his friend Lewis.

"Now," said Kit in a whisper, "let's make sure
of these first," and moving slowly forward, each
man riding one horse and leading another, they
once more reached the bank of the stream without
being discovered, and moving down it for about
half a mile, till they considered themselves out of
danger, they crossed and came to a halt.

"See here, Rose," said Kit, "this darned Injin
ain't satisfied. He wants more horses, and he won't
leave without 'em, and I suppose I'll have to see
him through; but we'll make sure of these, anyway.
You take four of 'em and clear out for the camp."

This matter being settled, Rose mounted his own
horse, and with Gale's mare beside him, and leading two others, he declared himself ready to start.

"Now, Rose," said Kit, "go slow for the first
mile or two, then make tracks for camp as fast as
ye can. When you get to the ridge cross it about
a mile below where we did. Now heave ahead, old
fellow, and we'll stay here till you get out of sight.
Tell the boys we're a comin'."

Rose, with his small drove of horses, started
across the plain, and was soon lost to view. After
riding about two miles he dismounted, and placing
his ear to the ground, listened intently for some

time, and hearing no sign of pursuit, he remounted and rode forward at a rapid pace. After crossing the ridge with some difficulty, on account of the numerous rocks, he once more reached the plain, and about two hours before daylight arrived safely at camp with four good horses, much to the astonishment as well as delight of his companions.

The next morning Kit Carson arrived safe in camp with but one horse, and it appeared to have been hard ridden. On being questioned, Kit said:

"It was all owin' to the Injun. He was too greedy—wanted too many horses—and the consequence was that when we started with about two dozen of 'em the rest all followed, and they got up a regular stampede. The Blackfeet got onter us, and we were obliged to cut and run. The red devils give us a pretty good chase, and just as we got to the ridge Jack's horse was wounded and he had to take to the rocks. I got safe to camp, but it was close shavin', I tell you."

The next morning Jack appeared in camp with two mules loaded with blankets, cloths, etc. It appeared that while the Blackfeet were searching for him among the rocks, he contrived to take the back track and returned to the Blackfoot camp, which he found deserted, except by a couple of mules which he found tied up there with their packs. With these he immediately started for the mountains, and by a route known only to the Indians, he managed to avoid his enemies and reach the camp in safety. A council was held the next day, and the trappers concluded that as the season was pretty far advanced and the Blackfeet were getting a little numerous, they would return to Ft. Hall and go into winter quarters.

CHAPTER VII.

IN WHICH ROSE AND HIS COMPANY RECEIVE
ANOTHER VISIT FROM THE BLACKFEET.

Rose and his party found they could no longer carry on their trapping expedition—the Indians having stripped them of everything. The nights were now getting very cold in the mountains, and as they were without blankets, and nearly out of ammunition, they concluded that their wisest plan would be to start at once for Fort Hall, and replenish their stores, as they were in no condition to face either the cold weather or the Indians, who were known to be at no great distance.

The party from the American Fur Company, who had been with them for the last four days, were about to return to their camp. The horses were brought in and loaded with skins and the trappers were smoking, laughing and chatting merrily prior to bidding each other adieu.

Two trappers, by the name of Meek and Leggit, had started on ahead, accompanied by Rose. They had just reached the top of a small bushy ridge and emerged into the open space beyond, when they saw a large band of Indians coming toward them. The trappers immediately turned and dashed into the bushes, and started for the camp as fast as their legs could carry them. The Indians, not being aware that the party of trappers they had fought a few days before had been strengthened and augmented by a party from the American Fur Company, came rushing on, and were within fifty yards of the camp before they discovered their mistake. The trappers were equally surprised to see a band of a hundred and fifty Blackfeet Indians rushing down upon them, yelling like demons. They were, however, equal to the emergency. Every man knew his duty and did his best to perform it.

The Indians came to a sudden halt, as twenty rifles poured their deadly fire among them, then letting fly a shower of bullets and arrows among the trappers, they at once took to the bushes, and now the fight commenced in earnest. Six of the Indians had been killed outright, and the trappers had three of their horses killed and three of their number were wounded. The Indians now rallied and fell back beyond the bushes in which the camp was situated, setting on fire the grass as they went. The fire quickly spread to the grove and shot up the pine trees in splendid columns of flame that seemed to lick the heavens. The Indians kept close behind the fire, shooting into the camp whenever they could approach near enough, the trappers replying by frequent volleys. The yells of the savages, the noise of the flames in the trees, the bellowing of the guns, whose echos rolled among the hills, and the excitement of a battle for life, made the scene one long to be remembered with distinctness.

Both sides fought with desperation. The Blackfoot blood was up—the trapper blood no less. As several of Gales' men had no ammunition they could do little more than take charge of the horses, which they led out into the bottom-land to escape the fire, fight the flames and look after the camp goods. Those who had some ammunition left showed the game spirit, and the fight became interesting as an exhibition of what mountain white men can do in a contest of one to ten, with the crack warriors of the red race. It was at any time a game party, consisting of Rose, Lewis, Meek,

Carson, Hawkins, Gale, Leggitt, Rider, Robinson, Anderson, Russell, Larrison, Ward, Parmaley, Wade, Michael, Head, and a few others whose names have been forgotten.

The trappers, being driven out of the grove by the fire, were forced to take to the open ground. The Indians, following the fire, had the advantage afforded by the shelter of the trees, and their shots made havoc among the horses, many of which were killed. As for the trappers, they used the horses for defence, making rifle pits behind them, when no other covert could be found. In this manner the battle was sustained until 3 o'clock in the afternoon, without loss of life to the whites, though several men were wounded.

Rose, whose ammunition had been exhausted, busied himself by keeping the horses out of danger and fighting the fire; having not only saved his own horse, but those belonging to Gale and Carson.

Just before 3 o'clock, Rose crept to the side of Carson, who was lying behind a dead horse, waiting for some Indian to expose enough of himself to be shot at, and asked him for a few rounds of ammunition. With this demand Carson at once complied, giving Rose half a dozen bullets and a part of his powder.

Rose pointed out to Carson a lot of scrubby pine

bushes, telling him if they could reach them they could flank the Indians, and stand a good chance to pick off several of them. Accordingly, Rose, Carson and Head left their "horse-fort," and creeping from bush to bush, contrived to reach the stunted pines before mentioned. Crawling through these for some little distance, they saw ten or a dozen Indians standing beneath a pine tree. They were not more than a hundred yards distant. Taking deliberate aim they fired, and with such good effect that the Indians scattered at once. The Blackfeet, finding that they were outflanked, or thinking, perhaps, a reinforcement had arrived, the chief ordered a retreat, calling out to the trappers that they would fight no more.

Bridger, who had started for the American Fur Company's camp the day before, was informed by two trappers who galloped into the camp, that a fight was going on between the Blackfeet and the trappers, about eighteen miles distant, on the north fork of the Gallatin. On hearing this he broke camp at once, and with his full force hurried to the scene of conflict, but did not arrive till the Blackfeet had made their retreat. They congratulated their friends on their success in having driven off the most warlike band of Indians that infest the mountain, and "they were sorry," as they expressed it, "that they did not get there till after the fun was over." They were, however, pretty well supplied with stores, and the wounded were at once attended to. Tents were pitched, beds were made out of dry grass and blankets, and their wounds were properly, if not scientifically, dressed. In some respects the Rocky Mountain trapper is very peculiar. He has an eye only to the reckless, the daring, the absurd, the humorous, and if any one of them is green enough to tell a tale of sorrow or misfortune, instead of meeting with sympathy and condolence, he is chaffed and joked by all of them, and this eventually proves to be the best tonic, as he soon begins to think his misfortunes not so bad as he at first thought, and in a short time will even laugh at them himself. Even in the midst of the deadly conflict, when the fire was roaring and crackling in every direction, and the bullets and arrows of their enemies flying among them, and the yells of a hundred and fifty blood-thirsty savages, eager for their lives, rent the air— even at such a time as this, loud bursts of laughter could be heard among the trappers as some witty sally met their ear, or some daring Indian was picked off by one of the white men and sent to the "happy hunting grounds."

Head, who, although a brave man, had a peculiar, nasal drawl when he spoke, which made all he said appear ludicrous, called one time in his slow, drawling tone: "I wish I could see the son of a gun that shot old Plute, (that was the name of his horse) I'd fix him!"

After this, when an Indian would expose himself, one of the trappers would call out, "there's the fellow that killed 'old Plute,' " and this sally would be followed by roars of laughter. This conduct may seem strange to many of our readers, who could scarcely believe that men in such imminent peril could be so reckless; but we beg leave to state that we write nothing but facts, furnished us by an eye-witness, and one who participated largely in the fight.

Had Bridger and his company arrived a few hours sooner they would have made short work of the Blackfeet, and their first intention was to follow them, but as so many of the trappers were wounded they thought it best to remain where they were till they became convalescent. In cases of emergency the Rocky Mountain trapper acts as both surgeon and nurse. One of the trappers was shot in the shoulder. Bridger having trimmed off a pine stick he probed the wound in order to find the locality of the ball. Ascertaining it was near the back part of the shoulder, he made an incision with his hunting knife, and with a piece of wire contrived to extricate the bullet. Covering the pine stick with a piece of cotton cloth, he ran it through the wound so as to remove anything of a poisonous nature. The shoulder was then dressed and bandaged. This surgical operation proved quite successful. In a few days the man was walking around with his arm in a sling, and soon after he completely recovered.

As the wounded men were now most of them convalescent it was agreed they should start at once for their winter quarters.

CHAPTER VIII.

IN WHICH THE TRAPPERS GO INTO WINTER QUARTERS ON SNAKE RIVER.

The trappers now commenced their preparations to cross the mountains and revisit Fort Hall, having concluded to make the neighborhood of that place their winter quarters.

The wounded were progressing favorably, with the exception of one, and this one we must now introduce to our readers.

The morning after the battle some of the trappers were searching among the bushes in order to discover how many Indians were killed, and if any were still living. In a small clump of pine bushes they discovered an Indian maiden, whose leg had been broken by a rifle ball, and who had crawled there to die. She was completely hidden, having covered herself with branches broken from the bushes around her, and this may probably account for her not having been seen by the Indians and taken away with them in their retreat. When she was first discovered by the trappers her leg was much swollen, and she was suffering the most excruciating agony, although she bore it with the heroism, or stoicism, peculiar to the Indian race. Her limb was dressed as tenderly, if not as skilfully, as a surgeon could have done it, and although at first it was generally supposed she would die from the effects of the wound, she began to slowly recover. The Indian village was but a few hundred yards from the battle ground, which will account for her being there.

Most of the trappers were wounded either in the head, arms or shoulders, and consequently as they became convalescent, their wounds did not interfere with their locomotion; but with the Indian maiden the case was different. Although in a few days she was able to sit up on her couch of skins, she could not walk a step, and the trappers found it necessary to improvise a litter, as they were determined to take their pet along with them—for a pet she had already become—and these rough but tender-hearted men vied with each other in their attempts to assist or amuse the poor little Indian maiden, whom they rescued from a fearful death. Her name was Chilsipee (the antelope), and the young girl soon became a pet and favorite with the whole company, and when the trappers started for Snake river, a sort of mattress was constructed from tent poles and buffalo robes, and fastened on a pack horse in such a manner that poor little Chilsipee could either lie down or sit up, and on the fourth day after they left the fork of the Gallatin they once more arrived safely at Fort Hall, Chilsipee and the wounded trappers standing the journey remarkably well.

A suitable spot was soon selected on the Snake river, above the Fort, to go into winter quarters. Lodges were at once erected, and everything done that was necessary to make their winter habitation comfortable, and now came the good time for the trappers. They had nothing to do but to eat, drink and be merry, and they did it to the fullest extent. Pasture was good and game abundant, and, to use a common expression, they "lived on the top of the pile."

In about two weeks Chilsipee was able to walk

around with the aid of a pair of crutches, which one of the men had made for her, and she now began to rapidly improve. The little Indian maiden was very industrious. Her dexterous and nimble fingers were never idle. She mended and patched for the whole camp, and she was kept busy making moccasins and leggings, at which she was an adept. Her lodge was the warmest and most comfortable in the camp, and the choicest portions of game were reserved for her use. Beads, trinkets and bright colored cloth were presented to her by the trappers, and it would not have been healthy for any one to hurt or injure her in any way. The trappers seemed determined to enjoy themselves to the utmost. Running, wrestling and jumping were the usual outdoor amusements, and when the weather was bad, cards, checkers and dominoes were resorted to. Often some one of the trappers would amuse his companions by relating some thrilling adventure. At other times songs would be sung, and the whole company would join in the chorus, and altogether they continued to have a lively and agreeable time. On the opposite side of the river timber was heavier and more plentiful than on the side they were encamped, and crossing in a "dug out" they would often make long excursions through the woods in search of game. One morning Rose and a trapper named Jack Larrison, paddled across the river in their canoe, and started for a small stream about four miles distant. After going up the stream for some little distance they saw a couple of fine elk feeding out on the prairie, but too far off for a shot. Knowing that if they were seen by the elk there would be no chance to get near enough to them, Rose volunteered to make a circuit so as to get around on the other side of them. He would then drive them toward Larrison, who was to remain hid in the bushes.

Rose crept through the long grass till the elk was between him and his companion. He then arose and walked toward them. As soon as the elk perceived him they started for the woods. When they came within range Larrison let fly at the buck, but, unfortunately, only wounded him, and the elk soon disappeared up the stream.

Determined not to be foiled, Rose and his companion followed the track of the elk, which they could easily do by the splashes of blood seen here and there on the ground. Late in the afternoon they came up with the wounded buck who was lying down. Larrison, thinking the buck was done for, drew his knife, but the animal suddenly sprang to his feet, striking Larrison on the leg with one of his immense antlers, cutting it severely, and nearly breaking the limb.

Rose, seeing his friend in danger, drew a bead on the animal, and shot it through the head, killing it instantly.

They were now, however, in a bad fix. Larrison's leg was badly hurt, and he could not walk a step, and they were at least eight or ten miles from the camp. Rose dressed the wound as well as he could, and it was agreed he should return to the camp and get assistance. Night was fast coming on, and in the distance Rose heard the howling of several wolves. Knowing it would not be safe to leave his wounded companion, he took him on his back and carried him to a safe distance from the dead elk, then gathering up some dry leaves and brush he soon had a roaring fire. This they kept up all night, while not far off they could hear the wolves howling and fighting over the dead body of the elk. The next morning Rose started for camp and soon returned with assistance, and Larrison was brought in, but it was several weeks before he recovered from the effects of that hunt.

Several severe snow storms occurred about Christmas time, and the snow at length became so deep that the trappers were compelled to strip cotton wood bark to feed their horses. After New

Year's, finding the snow, instead of decreasing, was getting deeper, the trappers resolved to break camp and move down to the Columbia river. The place they intended to stop at was Port Neuf. Not liking this location, however, they moved on down to Goose Creek, and no spot west of the mountains could have been found better adapted for winter quarters. The air was mild and balmy, and the broad surface of the Columbia river was covered with innumerable water fowl. Swans, geese, ducks and brandt could be seen by thousands swimming gracefully on the bosom of the stream, and although our trappers were not possessed of "purple and fine linen," they certainly fared sumptuously every day. Any amount of fish, especially speckled trout, could be had for the catching, and besides the water fowl, there was no lack of all kinds of game. The swan, however, seemed to be the favorite food with the trappers. They were large, fat and tender, some of them weighing over forty pounds. The swans were generally skinned and roasted. One of the trappers, a little more ingenious than the rest, manufactured a swan-skin cap. This, however, Chilsipee soon improved on. Picking out all the large feathers, and leaving nothing but the down, she made a very comfortable cap, which she presented to Rose on the 18th of February, he being twenty years of age on that day. As Isaac was a great favorite with the trappers a grand celebration was held on that day. Afterwards a shooting match, running, jumping and wrestling were resorted to, and at dinner time they partook of a feast fit for the gods. Buffalo rump, roast antelope, trout and swan figured largely in the entertainment, and Rose declares the celebration of his twentieth birthday to be one of the greatest and most pleasant eras in his life.

Toward the latter end of March they encountered two or three heavy storms of wind, rain and sleet, which they concluded to be the equinoctials, and after this fine weather began to set in and the trappers once more returned to their camp above Fort Hall.

CHAPTER IX.

IN WHICH THE AMERICAN FUR CO. LOSE THEIR HORSES.

March, which had been very stormy for that part of the country, began to assume a more favorable appearance. The sun came out warm and bright; the air was mild and balmy, and the snow was fast disappearing from the valleys, although in the mountains it was still quite deep. The men were now busy getting their traps ready for their usual spring campaign among the beaver, and everything around the camp began to show signs of renewed life and activity.

One day Mr. Wyeth called Rose to one side, and told him he had some thoughts of changing his occupation and going into some other business. He said he was in communication with the agents of the Hudson Bay Company, and that he thought of selling out to them. "I am aware," said Mr. Wyeth, "the other fur companies won't like it; but as Sublette and his company played me a mean trick, I shall consult only my own interests in this affair. And now, Rose," continued Wyeth, "I want you to stick to me; follow my fortunes, and I will make a man of you. I am aware that in your first season, instead of remaining a camp-keeper, as green hands generally do, you have become one of the most expert trappers in the company. You are an excellent shot, and, like an Indian, you can't be lost in either mountain, forest or prairie. These are grand qualifications in this western country, and I should like you to stay with me wherever I go, and you will lose nothing by it—depend on it. Take a few weeks to consider before making up your mind."

Rose promised to take the matter into consideration; but he had become so attached to this life of adventure, as well as to his companions, that he made up his mind at once not to accept Mr. Wyeth's offer; but if that gentleman should sell out to the Hudson Bay Company, he would join the American Fur Company, and his companions were much pleased with his decision.

Bridger's company had placed their horses on an island in the river. The pasture on the island was good, and the horses were considered safe from any bands of Indians who might be prowling around, and feeling satisfied with this the trappers neglected to watch them at night.

Early one morning the horses were missing from the island, and on examination it was discovered they had been stolen by a band of Blackfeet and driven up into the mountains. One of the animals was a famous horse belonging to Bridger, called Ogoroho. He was a splendid animal, and his owner valued him at three thousand dollars. He was considered the fastest horse on the Columbia river, and Bridger had won large sums of money with him at the rendezvous, where a good deal of horse-racing was generally carried on. Bridger was nearly wild over the loss of this noble animal, and about fifteen of the trappers immediately started in pursuit. The trail was easily followed, and they were soon once more among the snow.

This grew deeper and deeper as they advanced up the mountain, and Bridger and his company felt Confident they would soon come up with the Indians, as the horses could not travel much further on account of the deep snow.

About the middle of the day, Bridger, who was a tall, powerful man, and was walking along a little in advance of the company, saw smoke arising from among the cedar bushes, not more than two hundreds yards distant. They were compelled to walk in single file, as the snow was quite soft, and they sank in over their knees at every step. Bridger rushed forward, followed by his companions. The Blackfeet saw them approaching, and commenced at once putting on their snow-shoes. They were just eating dinner in an open space among the cedar bushes.

As soon as Bridger reached the open space he took deliberate aim at an Indian who was fitting an arrow to a bow, and shot him dead, and clubbing his rifle, he called out:

"Come on, boys, let's give them Hail Columbia!" then dashed forward about a rod in advance of the rest of the company; but the Indians, although over forty in number, did not stop to fight, but scooting off on their snow-shoes were soon hid among the cedar bushes, followed by several shots from the trappers, and now commenced what might be called a very unequal contest. The Indians out-numberd the trappers three to one, while with their snow shoes they could scoot around the white men in every direction.

The fight continued for several hours, the Indians keeping between the trappers and their horses, which had been driven higher up among the rocks.

Bridger and his party could make no advance, as the snow was so soft that they sank in over their knees at every step, and the Indians could not retreat with their horses, as it was impossible to drive them any further into the mountain on account of the deep snow.

Mark Head, who had accompanied Bridger's party, had loaned his rifle out the day before, and just before starting had secured an old flint-lock musket, and during the fight had ensconced him-self behind an old cedar stump. Here he was engaged in a duel with an Indian, who was hid behind a heavy bunch of cedar bushes about fifty yards distant. Here the Indian would load his fusee, sail out on his snow-shoes and blaze away at Mark Head, who would dodge behind the stump to avoid the shot; then a puff of smoke would be seen to curl up from the pan of his old musket but no report followed, for as Mark politely enpressed it, "the d—d thing wouldn't go off." After about three unsuccessful attempts, Head called out with a strong nasal twang: "See here, one of you fellows that's got a good gun, come and shoot this red relic of barbarism?"

Joe Lewis waded through the snow to where Head was lying, and the next time the Indian made his appearance Joe shot him dead.

In the meantime Bridger was nearly wild at the loss of his splendid animal, and his inability to reach the spot where the horses were concealed. Followed by Carson and Rose he had been pushing his way through a heavy growth of cedar bushes. Emerging into an open space he was suddenly confronted by half a dozen Indians on their snow-shoes. Their quick, guttural "Ugh! ugh!" had scarcely been uttered when Bridger and Carson fired simultaneously, knocking over two of their number. One of the Indians discharged his rifle at Carson, wounding him severely in the shoulder. (See Life of Kit Carson.)

Bridger had dashed back into the bushes to reload, knowing he was no match for the Blackfeet in their snow-shoes in a hand-to-hand fight. Two of the Indians, seeing Carson was wounded, rushed forward to finish him, when Rose, who had been a few yards in the rear, put in an appearance, and, seeing at once how matters stood, shot the foremost Indian. The other raised his tomahawk, and was about to dash out Carson's brains when Rose suddenly sprang forward and dealt him a heavy blow in the breast with the butt of his rifle and rendered him *hors-de-combat*. Bridger and Rose then assisted Carson to the rear, where his wound was bandaged as well as it could be till they reached camp, and, as night was coming on, it was thought best to retreat, procure snow-shoes and reinforcements, and endeavor to regain their horses.

The next morning, the trappers, forty in number, well armed and with snow-shoes, started up the hollow toward the Indian encampment, determined, if possible, to make sure of their animals this time. One of the trappers, who was in advance, saw a beaver among the cedars near the bank of the stream, and shot it, and this proved to be an unlucky shot for the party, as it afterward appeared. The Indians were coming towards them with their horses, but, on hearing the shot, they turned off, and, making a detour, came in behind the trappers, and taking the back track soon reached the plains. As soon as Bridger and his party reached the place where the Indians had turned off they knew at once what had occurred, and hurried back to camp, but too late. Indians and horses had disappeared, and Bridger and his company never saw them again. The trappers at first concluded to follow on the Indian trail, but as the weather now set in warm, and their busy time was coming, they concluded to break camp at once and commence operations.

CHAPTER X.

IN WHICH ROSE AND HIS COMPANY GO TO SALT RIVER—ATTACKED BY BLACKFEET.

Bridger and his companions felt very sore over the loss of so many of their best horses; but more especially did the bushway, Bridger, mourn the loss of his gallant steed and far-famed racer, Ogoroho. His owner would have fought the Blackfeet every day for a month if by that means he could have regained possession of his noble animal, but Ogoroho was a thing of the past—Bridger never saw him again.

The trappers still had a goodly number of horses, and some of the Nez Perces and Flathead Indians having heard the company wished to purchase more horses, soon brought a drove of them to camp, and the trappers selected from them enough to make up their full complement; but the snow was getting so soft in the mountains that it would be impossible to cross the eastern slope for some time, and as they intended to do their spring trapping on the tributaries of the Missouri river, or the streams running into Salt Lake, they concluded to wait till the route became passable.

In the meantime matters were progressing favorably in camp. Chilsipee had nearly recovered from her wound, and as the trappers had striven hard through the winter to teach her the English language, she could now converse quite freely, although in a very broken and disjointed way. On being asked by one of the trappers to tell her age, she pointed to the grass, which was now getting quite green, and counted thirteen on her fingers, giving them to understand this was the thirteenth spring she had seen. She related in her broken way many anecdotes of skirmishes her nation had had with the white people and also with the other Indian nations, and she appeared to be as happy as the day was long. She lodged with some of the free-trappers' wives, but was always ready and willing to make herself useful as nurse, cook or seamstress, or in any way in which her services would be of use to the trappers. Kit Carson was getting on as well as could be expected. One or two pieces of bone had worked out, but being in his left shoulder, his wound did not disable him as badly as it might have done.

In the latter part of April Bridger concluded to cross the mountains to their spring trapping grounds. His route was by what was then known as the Tetons' Pass. The Tetons are three lofty peaks in the mountains, whose tops are nearly always hid in the clouds. These peaks serve as a good land-mark for the trappers for many miles around. On the last of April, Bridger, with the most of his company, started for the Tetons' Pass, leaving the remainder of the company, fifteen in number—among whom were Rose and Lewis—to try their luck on the tributaries of the Snake river, and after trapping there for some time, they were to cross the mountains at a more southern point and join the company on Bear river.

Rose and his party at once started for their intended hunting grounds and the the third morning after leaving camp they reached the banks of the Salt river. The stream was full from bank to bank, owing to the late rains and the melting snow, and although not more than twenty-five or thirty yards wide it was impossible to ford it. They were compelled to cross, however, as they could not ascend the side they were on owing to the steepness of the mountain, while on the other side it was a level plain for some distance. Spreading one of their lodges on the ground, their traps and goods were placed upon it, and the buffalo-skin lodge was securely wrapped around them. Two or three huge packs were in this manner constructed and tied in such a way that no water could penetrate them. A couple of trappers then swam their horses across the stream, carrying with them the end of a rope. The packs were then launched into the stream and drawn to the other side. In the meantime the balance of the horses and men got safely across. They had scarcely drawn the last pack across and opened it when their ears were saluted with the well-known blood-curdling war-whoop of the Blackfeet, who appeared, about fifty in number, on the side of the stream they had just left. The Indians had been following their trail the whole day and if they had come up half an hour before every trapper would have been killed, as all their rifles and ammunition were securely fastened in their pack. No sooner, however, did the war cry of the savages fall upon their ear, accompanied by a shower of bullets from their fusees (this being the only kind of firearms the Indians had at that time) than the trappers at once seized their rifles, and taking their horses to a safe distance, they took shelter among the stumpy pines that skirted the stream, and the battle commenced in good earnest. One of the trappers, a young man named St. Clair, was badly scared, this being his first fight with the Indians. Handing his rifle to a Nez Perces Indian, half-a-dozen of whom accompanied the trappers, he commenced digging a hole behind the bushes with his hunting knife in which to shelter himself from the bullets that were flying around him. The Blackfeet would gallop close to the edge of the river on the other side, then wheel and retreat as rapidly as they came. At each of these charges the trappers would generally bring down one or two of their assailants. As the Indians came up St. Clair would duck his head into the small hole he had dug, it not being big enough to contain the rest of his body, and he would keep it there till the Indians retreated, much to the amusement of his companions. The Nez Perces Indian who had St. Clair's rifle, after discharging it, attempted to reload by first ramming down the bullet, thus rendering the rifle useless during the rest of the fight. As the Indians had not made their appearance for some time Rose determined to reconnoiter. Accordingly, taking with him his trusty rifle, he climbed to the top of a pine tree close by. Looking around in every direction he was astonished to perceive, not more than thirty yards distant, an Indian on the same side of the river as himself, crawling through the grass. He had, apparently, swam the river, and was, when seen by Rose, throwing stones at three or four horses belonging to the trappers, with the intention of driving them farther away from the camp. Rose laid his rifle out on a limb, and taking deliberate aim, blazed away. That Indian never threw another stone. Dropping down from the tree, lest he might become a target, he reloaded his rifle, and waiting some considerable time, again ascended the tree. About a hundred yards distant on the other side of the river he saw ten or twelve Indians closely huddled together, apparently in deep consultation. Resting his rifle on a limb, he let drive among them. The shot caused them to scatter in every direction; but Rose did not stop to see what damage it had done. Knowing it would not be healthy to remain in the pine, he dropped his rifle, muzzle downwards, to the ground, and he himself quickly followed.

The fight lasted several hours, but, toward evening, the Blackfeet disappeared. The trappers camped on the spot all night, keeping a bright lookout; but they were not molested, and the next morning they packed their horses and started up the stream, and the day following reached one or two of the tributaries on which they intended to commence trapping.

A spot was selected for the camp, and tents were erected, and while the camp-keepers and Indians were busy getting things in order, Rose strolled to a small hill about fifty yards distant. From this spot he saw a large bunch of willows and cedars further up the stream. Thinking it a good place for a beaver dam he walked toward it. While passing a bunch of willows he heard a savage growl, and turning quickly, saw an enormous grizzly bear not more than fifteen feet distant. The animal had reared on its hind legs, and for one moment Rose and the bear stood face to face. He was unarmed. He had left his rifle at the camp, and as the bear with a savage growl came toward him he thought "discretion the better part of valor," and started at the top of his speed for a pine tree about thirty yards distant. Rose says he feels confident he sprang five or six feet up into that tree, and catching a limb swung himself out of the bear's reach; but not one moment too soon, as the grizzly was close behind him, and rearing up it tore off every limb it could reach in its fury. He would then walk around the tree growling fiercely. He would then rear up again and try to reach his intended victim.

Rose would occasionally break off a limb and throw it down. This the bear would seize and savagely tear to pieces. At length his female companion made her appearance. Mr. Grizzly started to meet her, and the two wandered away up stream. Rose at once returned to camp, and from that time forward never started on any expedition without taking with him his trusty rifle.

CHAPTER XI.

IN WHICH THEY COMMENCE THEIR SPRING TRAPPING. A TRIP TO THE DIGGER COUNTRY.

Trapping now commenced in good earnest. Beaver were plenty, and there seemed to be every prospect of a favorable spring hunt.

Rose had concluded not to accept Mr. Wyeth's offer, although he had no doubt it would have been advantageous so to do. He was too much attached to his present occupation and to the men with whom he had shared so many dangers, so that he was easily induced to join the American Fur Company, which he was at full liberty to do, Mr. Wyeth having sold out to the Hudson Bay Company.

This leaving one company and joining another was effected without any financial settlement by the trapper. His name and accounts were transferred from the books of one company to the books of the other, and the clerks settled the matter between themselves.

As I have before stated, Rose was not an educated man, having never gone beyond "baker" in the spelling-book. The multiplication table was still above his comprehension, and the "rule of three" was to him downright Greek. Now, although Rose was not a proficient in book learning, he certainly had studied the habits and propensities of the beaver, more carefully and successfully than any other man in the company. So well did he understand the movements of these little animals that he knew exactly where to set his traps, and before the spring campaign was over he was pronounced the most expert and successful trapper in the company. He was full of energy and ambition and proud of his success as a trapper, and he would often start off on a hunting expedition for days alone, and generally having a good pack of beaver skins to show on his return to camp.

After trapping in their present location about three weeks they were joined by Mr. Dripps, one of the head men and owners of the American Fur Company, who informed them that all matters relating to the transfer had been settled with Mr.

Wyeth, and that, consequently, all those who had formerly belonged to Wyeth's company were now attached to the American Fur Company. He also gave orders to join Bridger at once, and the next morning the trappers started for Cache Valley, where Bridger was then located. The boys were rejoiced to meet with each other again, and some little time was spent in hearing and relating anything of interest that had occurred during their separation.

A band of Utah Indians were encamped on the river a short distance below. These Indians were generally known by the trappers as the "Utes." They were a friendly tribe and well disposed toward the whites, who often found them very serviceable.

One morning as the trappers were preparing to visit their traps they were astonished to see a large grizzly bear walking leisurely toward the camp and not more than three hundred yards distant. When he first caught sight of the trappers he paused for a few seconds, as though to make a reconnoisance, then growling fiercely he came boldly on as if determined to do battle with the whole camp. Some of the boys thought this a good opportunity to have some sport, and, leaving their rifles in camp, mounted their horses, and borrowing some bows and arrows from the Utes, they started out to meet their grizzly foe. Two of the trappers galloped around the bear, one on each side of him, and, suddenly wheeling, they each rode close enough to shoot an arrow into the monster. Not being very proficient with this kind of weapon their arrows did not penetrate the body of the bear more than an inch or two. This only served to make him furious, and with a savage growl he gave chase to the nearest horseman. Another trapper would then shoot an arrow into him, and the grizzly would turn at once and give chase to his new adversary. This sport was kept up until about fifty arrows were sticking in the bear, not one of them inflicting a wound deep enough to be mortal.

One of the Ute Indians now rode up, and with his bow and arrows shot the bear through the lungs, putting an end to the animal and the sport at the same time.

The .Utes having informed the trappers that beaver were very plentiful on the Humboldt river, Bridger concluded to start for that section at once, and the necessary preparations were accordingly made for the journey. Their route lay through what was known as the Digger country, a barren and arid desert, in which it was known no game of any consequence could be found, and the company set to work at once to prepare provisions for the journey. A number of buffalo were shot and the meat smoked and dried, and the Utes were set to work to gather the yampa, tobacco and camerass roots. These were beaten into a pulp and afterward formed into cakes and dried in the sun. They were found to be very nourishing and not at all unpalatable. Having gathered as much provisions together as they thought would do them till they reached the Humboldt or some other place where a fresh supply could be procured, they started off in good spirits for their new trapping grounds.

Nothing of interest occurred till after crossing the Owyhee, when they struck the desert before mentioned. The plains here are covered with a sort of alkaline matter resembling cakes of salt. Some of these were the color of sassafras, while others were purely white. No kind of vegetation could anywhere be seen but few wild sage and grease bushes, and not a living animal larger than a lizard could be found in any direction. To make the matter still more unpleasant there was no water, and the poor animals, after traveling all day, were compelled to camp all night without being able to quench their thirst. The next day the march was resumed, and as the sun rose high in the heavens the thirst of men and animals became almost intolerable, and still before them extended what appeared to be an endless waste of white, salty looking matter, from which as they traveled along a sort of dust would arise that got into the eyes and mouths of both man and beast making them nearly crazy. Toward noon the heat became oppressive, and with parched throats and swollen tongues the bravest among the trappers began to wish they had not undertaken the journey. Toward nightfall, they came to a sort of swampy place on the plains. No sooner did the mules feel their feet sinking into the mud than they set up a bray that could be heard for miles, and dashing forward to where the mud was the softest they commenced eating and sucking at it as if it was the most delicious thing they had ever tasted in their lives. Several holes were at once scooped out, the men working with their knives and hands, and these were soon filled with thick muddy water, and although it had an earthy, rooty, brackish taste, the men and animals contrived to satisfy the cravings of thirst for that time. The next day they reached the Humboldt river and commenced trapping.

The tributaries of the Humboldt did not answer their expectations. Beaver were not at all plentiful, and no game of any description could anywhere be found, and provisions soon began to run low. At first they tried to eat the flesh of the beaver, but this was soon discovered to be poisonous, from the fact the beaver feeds on the wild parsnip, which abounds on the Humboldt river. Besides this they were much annoyed by the Digger Indians. These little savages, who come nearer supplying Darwin's missing link than any other human beings on the face of the globe, are low in stature, being not more than four feet in height. They have scarcely any foreheads and their teeth are worn to the gums with eating roots. Their only arms consist of a bow and arrow, and the only reason why they have not been wiped out of existence is from the fact that they are surrounded by so arid and sterile a region that no other tribe of Indians can get at them. Besides the roots their food consists of lizards, grasshoppers, crickets and ants, which they devour greedily. Some of these savage little imps would steal up close to the camp in the night, and shoot one of the horses or mules and in a few days afterward, when the company had moved farther up stream, the Diggers would pounce upon the decomposed body of the animal, and in a few hours nothing but the well picked bones could be found. This shooting had become so frequent that a guard had to be stationed every night.

One morning a big Spaniard belonging to the company, named Masselleno, saw one of the Diggers creeping toward the horses. As soon as the Indian found he was discovered he started to run. Masselleno galloped after him, and casting his lasso, at which he was an adept, he caught the Digger around the neck, then wheeling his horse galloped with him through the grease bushes so that when brought in the savage was nearly torn to pieces.

As beaver were not very plentiful, and as there was neither grass nor cotton wood for the horses, and no game of any description, Bridger concluded to return to their former trapping ground and once more breaking camp, after innumerable hardships, they again arrived in the land of plenty, but the season was too far advanced for trapping, and Bridger and his company commenced making preparations to start for the rendezvous.

CHAPTER XII.

IN WHICH ROSE RUNS A RACE—CHILSIPEE PREPARES FOR THE RENDEZVOUS.

Rose and his company presented a very dejected and forlorn appearance on their return from the

Humboldt river. Their faces were pale and haggard, and their forms attenuated by famine and fatigue. Nor were their animals in any better condition. In fact, their trip into the Digger country came near using them up.

Before leaving Snake river Rose had purchased a horse—the first one he had ever owned—and either by good luck or good judgment, or perhaps by both combined, he contrived to become the possessor of one of the best horses in the company. He was an excellent saddle horse and hard to beat in a race, and it was owing to this fact that Chilsipee chose it as her favorite riding animal.

When the Indian maiden wanted a horse to ride it was only necessary for her to express the desire, as no trapper ever thought of refusing her.

While trapping on the Humboldt river the horse belonging to Rose would run loose about the camp, and as it was quite gentle, and a great favorite with Chilsipee, she would walk a long distance to get grass for it, or any stray bunches of cotton wood that could be found, and the consequence was that when they returned to Cache Valley this animal was in better condition than any other horse in the company.

The camp occupied by Bridger and his company, near the mouth of Bear river, could not have been better selected. After their long and arduous journey from the Digger country, the spot was well calculated to recruit the strength of their nearly starving and exhausted animals. The fogs arising from Salt Lake seemed materially to assist the growth of vegetation. The grass was green and plentiful, and the horses were improving every day; but, owing to the fact that a band of Indians had been camping in the vicinity previous to the arrival of our trappers, game appeared to be very scarce. Accordingly, Kit Carson, who had purchased a couple of horses from some Nez Perces Indians, pursuaded Rose to accompany him on a hunting excursion to the headwaters of Snake river, where buffalo were said to be plentiful. The two men started on their hunt, each leading a pack-horse, and camped the first night on one of the tributaries of Bear river. The next morning they struck across for the headwaters of Snake river, and about noon had the good fortune to kill two buffalo. These were skinned and dressed, and the meat packed on the lead horses. In the afternoon, after riding up the bank of a small stream, Kit Carson suddenly stopped, declaring he could smell smoke. Rose dismounted, and climbing to the top of a small hill, discovered a camp of Indians, a little way up the stream. Returning he informed

Kit there was no danger as the Indians were Snake Diggers, these Indians being not at all warlike, and generally on friendly terms with the white men.

The two hunters started at once for the Indian camp and when within two hundred yards of it a young Indian girl, who had been watching their approach, started from a clump of bushes, and ran like a deer to join her companions, her long, black hair streaming behind her in the wind. She was apparently about fifteen years of age, small, graceful and active as a fawn, and Carson declared she was the prettiest Indian squaw he had ever seen.

"I'm goin' to make a dicker fur that gal," exclaimed Kit. "I'll have her if it takes the best horse I've got," and the men at once rode forward toward an old Indian, who appeared to be the chief, and Kit commenced, by signs and what little Indian language he understood, to make the old chief understand what was required.

The maiden was at once brought forward. In person she was small, but exquisitely proportioned, and her eyes were large and brilliant. She wore a dress of deer skin, that reached just below her knees, the upper part of it resembling what is known as a "butcher's apron." Her arms and shoulders were bare, and leggings and moccasins of deer skin completed her attire. After some little pow-wowing, the chief agreed to sell his daughter for a horse and a red blanket, and Kit, placing his new purchase on a pack-horse, in company with Rose, started for camp with his dusky bride.

Jack Robinson, had married a squaw from the same tribe, his wife being known among the trappers as "Madame Jack." She, together with Chilsipee, took, "Madame Kit" in hands, and soon had her dressed in a manner becoming the wife of a free trapper, and "Madame Kit" and "Madame Jack" were soon the best of friends.

Bridger had for some time noticed two or three islands situated a considerable distance out on the lake. One day he ascended a small hill and surveyed the largest of these islands with a spy-glass. He plainly saw several small streams running down the declivity, and concluded it would be a good place for beaver. In order to ascertain if he was correct in his idea he inquired of several of the Indians who were camping with them, but they could give him no information. An old Indian told him he had known the islands for a long time, but did not think they had ever been visited by trappers. Bridge at length concluded to go on a voyage of discovery, and the men soon constructed two rafts, Traps and provisions were placed on them and with the aid of poles, they commenced their voyage. After polling out into the lake for some distance, the water became so deep, that their poles were no longer of any use to them, and a fresh wind springing up at that time, there was every prospect of their being blown out into the lake. After drifting two or three miles, with no chance to help themselves, except by using their poles as paddles, they fortunately struck a shallow place in the lake and soon polled themselves to the shore, and their voyage to the island was given up for that time.

Game having for some time been a little scarce in the neighborhood of the camp, they were much pleased one morning when a hunter informed them he had seen a herd of buffalo feeding on the plain a few miles distant, and Rose, in company with several other trappers, mounted their horses and started in search of the game. Rose had often shot buffalo in what is known as a "still hunt," or "approach." This mode of hunting is performed on the prairie by getting down in the long grass and creeping close enough to the animal to get a shot. Rose was considered quite an expert at this. Dressed in his wolf-skin cap with a wolf's ear standing up on each side of it, he would crawl through the long grass, and if the buffalo saw him at all they would take him to be a coyote and go on feeding till they were knocked over by a ball from his unerring rifle. But Rose was now to experience for the first time the excitement of a buffalo hunt on horseback, and feeling confident that he was better mounted than any of his companions he determined to distinguish himself. To this he was urged on by the remarks of his fellow trappers.

"Boys," said Carson, "there's no use in tryin'; Rose is goin' to have the first buffalo, I'll bet on that."

"Yes," replied Larrison, "that 'ere critter of his'n is a leetle too fast for anything here."

"Look at him!" exclaimed Head. "He'll be among them buffler before they can get a chance to stampede," and this really seemed to be the case. They had now arrived within a short distance of the herd which began to show signs of disquiet, when Rose, urged on by the remarks of his friends, dashed toward them at a furious rate, far outstripping his companions. As he drew near the herd they at first huddled together, as if panic stricken. A large old buffalo bull, in attempting to fly had fallen to the ground, and as Rose and his horse came up at head-long speed, they pitched over the fallen animal, and Rose, turning one or two somersaults, came heavily to the ground, about a rod in advance of his horse. Springing to his feet and finding he was not hurt, he was looking around for his rifle, when to his horror he perceived that the buffalo bull had also regained his feet, and with glaring eyes, lowering head, and a roar like a tornado, was coming toward him. Rose was a good runner, and now commenced a very exciting race. For about one hundred yards it was nip and tuck, the horns of the infuriated animal being sometimes within a foot of our hero's body. Some of the trappers who witnessed the race shouted: "Go it, Rose!" while the strong nasal drawl of Mark Head could be heard roaring out: "Go it, buffler!" Rose, finding the animal getting a little too close, took off his wolf-skin cap and striking behind him as he ran hit the buffalo on the nose. Rose redoubled his exertions, and he ran thirty or forty rods further at a killing pace, when, turning his head, he was astonished to find the bull had given up the chase and had started off after his companions. Rose went back and picked up his rifle, but his horse was nowhere to be seen, it having gone off with the herd of buffalo. Shots and shouts were occasionally heard and our hero, following on the trail, was soon busy skinning and cutting up the meat of the animals slain by his

companions. In a few hours the trappers returned
loaded with meat, and to the great delight of Rose,
bringing with them his horse, which he had given
up as lost. The trappers enjoyed a hearty laugh
at his expense, and he soon discovered that,
knowing his inclination to be always foremost in
any hunting or trapping expeditions, the boys
had made use of the expressions before mentioned
to urge him on and get him into a snap something
like the one his head-long rush had led him into.

The time for the rendezvous was now drawing
near, and this is an era in the life of the Rocky
Mountain trapper. It is the great oasis in the
desert of his existence, and is to him what the
"Jubilee" was to the bondmen of old. The stock
of goods laid in at the last rendezvous had for
some time been exhausted. Their blankets were
worn and tattered, their ammunition was getting
scarce, and they were out of tobacco. Besides this
they had heard nothing from home or the haunts
of civilization for many months, and any of my
readers can realize how a company arriving from
St. Louis, bringing with them an abundance of
goods and news from home would be welcomed by
these hearty and isolated men. The trappers were
making great preparations for the coming rendezvous, and Chilsipee had been busily engaged all

winter and spring in preparing for this momentous occasion. The news came at last that the company from St. Louis had arrived, and the trappers started for the rendezvous. As soon as they came within a few miles of the place they formed themselves into line, the head bushway taking the lead, the free trappers coming next in order, these were succeeded by the camp-keepers leading the pack horses loaded with skins, and the animals loaded with the lodges and lodge poles, together with the squaws, brought up the rear.

Chilsipee was in the height of her glory, and she was indeed a picture worthy the pencil of one of the greatest masters. Her horse, the one belonging to Rose, was beautifully and tastefully caparisoned. A broad leathern belt, a foot wide, reached from the saddle across its breast; this was covered with fine red cloth, and tastefully ornamented with beads, which were worked into stars and other emblematical devices. Porcupine quills also formed part of the decorations, and the whole was fringed with a large number of girlews or small bells which yielded a jingling, musical sound as she galloped along. Her saddle and saddle cloth were ornamental in a similar manner; but Chilsipee herself was a picture; her fine beaver skin cap was bound with gold lace and girlews; her tight-fitting bodice was of the finest red cloth, worked with beads and porcupine quills; her flowing blue skirt was also of the finest material, and this together with her red leggings and moccasins, like the rest of her dress, was elaborately embroidered. She rode as all Indian women do, man fashion, and the trappers were all delighted with and proud of their little pet. Chilsipee would ride at the head of the column, then, on rising ground, she would halt her horse and allow the calvacade to pass by, like an army passing in review before a general. Then, starting from the rear, she would gallop to the front at full speed, amid shouts of: "Hurrah! for Chilsipee." "Go it, little un'!"

The rendezvous was quite an exciting picture; all the friendly Indians and trappers for hundred of miles around would be there, bringing in their skins and horses to trade, and white men, Indians, squaws and children, to the number of eight hundred or a thousand could often be found there, and sometimes as high as two thousand horses and mules.

As soon as the trappers had laid in their necessaries, such as ammunition, blankets and tobacco, they commenced enjoying themselves. Alcohol could be bought at four dollars a pint, and the trappers, after their long abstinence, would indulge freely. Horse-racing, foot-racing, wrestling, jumping, and all kinds of manly sports were continually going on, and fun and frolic appeared to be the order of the day. Many of the trappers would spend in a few weeks all they had earned in a year; but being now supplied with necessaries, they looked forward to the future boldly and hopefully.

> Although no rich viands were found at their board,
>   They caroled away idle sorrow;
> With pleasure they take what to-day may afford,
>   And look forward with hope for to-morrow.

CHAPTER XII.

IN WHICH THE RENDEZVOUS IS VISITED BY MISSIONARIES—A FIGHT WITH THE BANNOCKS.

The rendezvous of the Rocky Mountain Company seldom took place without combining with its many wild elements some of the other more civilized and refined. Artists, botanists, travelers and hunters from the busy world outside the wilderness frequently claimed the companionship, if not the hospitality, of the fur companies in their wanderings over prairies and among mountains; but this year they were to have visitors differing from any before mentioned. This year there appeared at the rendezvous two gentlemen, who had accompanied the St. Louis company on its outward trip to the mountains, whose object was not the procurement of pleasure or the improvement of science. They had come to found missions among the Indians; the Rev. Samuel Parker and Rev. Dr. Marcus Whitman.

The cause which had brought these gentlemen to the wilderness was a little incident connected with the fur trade. Four Flathead Indians, in the year 1832, having heard of the Christian religion from the few devout men connected with the fur companies, formed a winter journey to St. Louis, and there made injuiry about the white man's religion. This incident soon became noised abroad and was taken up by the churches. The Methodist church was the first to respond. When Wyeth returned to the mountains in 1834 two missionaries accompanied him, destined for the valley of the Willamette river, in Oregon.

The appearance of the reverend gentlemen among them at the rendezvous did not interfere with the fun and frolics of the trappers; they continued to enjoy themselves as only men can do who meet together for a short space of time, once in a year. A good beaver skin would purchase a quart of alcohol, and this would make a good treat for a lodge. Sometimes each member of a lodge would purchase a quart of flour, for which they paid one dollar. This was all put together in a camp-kettle, mixed with water and a little salt, then made up into cakes and baked on the coals; but this was an extravagance and a luxury the ·trappers seldom indulged in.

There are two months in the year in which beaver skins are not considered marketable; the beaver shedding his fur about that time, and it is in these months, July and August, the rendezvous is always held.

Among the numerous tribes of friendly Indians who came in from the mountains to trade with the white men there was at present assembled the Nez Perces, the Flatheads, the Delawares and the Snake Indians. Besides these, there was a large tribe called the Bannocks camped about four or five miles below the rendezvous.

These Indians were war-like and ferocious and not altogether to be trusted; but as they were well provided with excellent horses they often came into camp to sell or trade their animals.

One day a Bannock and a Nez Perces had made a horse trade. After some time the Bannock came to the conclusion he had got the worst of the bargain, and insisted the Nez Perces should give him back his horse. This the Indian refused to do, and the Bannock chief went back to his tent vowing vengeance. The next morning great preparations were going on in the Bannock camp; the warriors were all assembled, and it was evident their intentions were by no means of a peaceful character. They commenced daubing themselves and their horses with war paint, which gave them a most grotesque and ferocious appearance.

They then mounted and started for the rendezvous, and reaching the camp they rode through it in a most taunting and insulting way. The chief was mounted on a fine gray horse, which was painted in an extraordinary manner. On its breast dark red spots were painted to imitate bullet wounds. From these, red streaks of vermilion were drawn like the flowing of blood. The same marks were on the animal's neck and other parts of his body. On reaching the middle of the camp they commenced their war-dance. After going through with this fantastic performance they remounted their horses and just at this time the Nez Perces, who had made the horse trade, rode up and was immediately recognized by the Bannock chief, who, without hesitation, immediately raised his rifle and shot him dead.

Bridger, who had been watching the proceeding, expecting it would end in a row, roared out in his stentorian voice: "Yer guns, men! Every man to his gun!" and the trappers immediately commenced arming themselves.

Rose had just emerged from his lodge armed with his rifle. The Bannock chief came galloping by; he was evidently wounded in the head, and when the horse came in front of the lodge he was struck by a rifle ball and fell, pinning his rider to the earth by one of his legs. The Bannock raised his hand to wipe the flow of blood out of his eyes. That moment a Delaware Indian seeing his situation, sprang toward him, tomahawk in hand. Rose was standing within six feet of the wounded Indian, and as the Bannock saw his enemy, the Delaware, approaching, the intense look of supplication or entreaty he cast upon Rose he thinks will haunt him until his dying day. At first he felt inclined to interfere and save the Bannock; but before he had time to consider, the Delaware drove his tomahawk deep into his enemy's skull, and not being able to jerk it out, he seized the handle with both hands, placed his foot on the dying man's head and gave it a wrench that tore away a portion of the skull, then, with a whoop and a yell, he started away in search of another victim.

The Bannocks retreated toward their camp,

firing indiscriminately at both white men and Indians, and the Delawares and Nez Perces, together with some of the trappers, soon procured horses and followed them to their camp. Here the fight continued the balance of the day. Toward night the trappers and Nez Perces returned to their rendezvous, leaving the Delawares to watch their enemies.

These Delawares were the remnant of a once powerful tribe, who formerly belonged to Western New York or Northern Ohio. They were well armed with rifles, and were considered the best marksmen at the rendezvous.

The Bannocks, soon discovering they had now but a few Delawares to contend with, mounted their horses and charged upon them, and the Delawares, being outnumbered, were compelled to retreat, and a running fight was kept up for some time.

A young Delaware boy, by the name of Jonas, was in the rear of the retreating tribe. He was a brave little fellow, about fourteen years of age, and was very much liked by the white men, who had taught him to speak their language. Unfortunately a ball from a Bannock rifle broke a leg of the animal he was riding, and Jonas was compelled to dismount and run for it. Finding, however, that it would be impossible for him to escape, the brave little fellow wheeled about and faced the advancing foe. Kneeling on one knee, he took deliberate aim with his rifle, and waiting till the nearest Indian came within twenty feet of him he shot him dead. The next morning the trappers, in company with the Delawares went to the spot and found the body of poor Jonas, scalped, and literally cut to pieces. The trappers were so much enraged that they joined with the Delawares and Nez Perces in another attack on the Bannocks; but on reaching the camp of the latter it was found they had taken shelter on an island. The upper part of this island was covered with drift-timber, behind which the Indians ensconced themselves. The trappers and their allies were posted among the bushes on the banks of the river, and whenever a Bannock would show himself he was very apt to get a quietus from one of their bullets. In this way the fight continued several hours. Rose, who was moving down the river in the shelter of the bushes, came upon Kit Carson and a trapper by the name of Meek, who were discussing the possibility of making a raid on the island.

The Bannocks had a large number of horses, and some of these had strayed to the lower end of the island. Meek said he would contrive to engage the attention of the Bannocks, while Rose and Carson conducted the raid, the object being to drive over as many of the enemy's horses as they could surround. Accordingly, when the signal was given, Rose, Carson, and a trapper by the name of Crow, and about a dozen Delawares, mounted, swam over to the island and succeeded in capturing about forty of their horses. With these they returned to camp, thinking the Bannock's sufficiently punished.

In a few days Mr. Dripps, the traveling partner of the American Fur Company, started with about one hundred and fifty horses and mules, heavily ladened with beaver skins, for St. Louis, and the homeward bound company carried with them many letters, messages and commissions from the friends they left behind. When the time arrived for the trappers to start on their fall hunt, Bridger informed them that a prize of three hundred dollars would be given to the trapper whose record proved he had taken the most beaver skins during the year. As soon as Rose heard of this he determined to win the prize, if within the bounds of possibility. How he succeeded, time will show.

CHAPTER XIV.

IN WHICH THE FIRST SERMON IN THE ROCKY
MOUNTAINS WAS BROKEN UP BY A HERD OF
BUFFALO. CALEB WILKINS AND
THE GRIZZLY.

Shortly after the arrival of Messrs. Parker and Whitman the rendezvous broke up. A party to which Rose was attached moved in the direction of the Snake river headwaters, the missionaries accompanying them, and after making two camps, came, on Saturday evening, to Jackson's Little Hole, a small mountain valley, near the larger one commonly known as Jackson's Big Hole.

On the following day Joe Meek went around among the trappers and informed them that religious services were to be held.

As a general thing the trappers knew nothing about Sunday, and the only way they had of ascertaining the day of the month was when they had an opportunity of referring to the company's books. Preacher Parker, being fresh from the States, still kept the run of the Sabbath, and it was from this knowledge preaching was announced for that day.

A scene more unusual could hardly have transpired than that of a company of trappers listening to the preaching of the word of God. Very little pious reverence marked the countenance of that wild and motley congregation. Curiosity, incredulity, sarcasm, or a mocking levity were more plainly perceptible in the expression of the men's faces than either devotion or the longing expectancy of men habitually deprived of what they once highly valued. The Indians alone showed by their eager listening that they desired to become acquainted with the mystery of the "Unknown God."

The Rev. Samuel Parker preached and the men were as politely attentive as it was in their reckless nature to be, until, in the midst of the discourse, a herd of buffalo appeared in the valley, when the congregation incontinently broke up without staying for a benediction, and every man made haste after his horse, gun and rope, leaving Mr. Parker to discourse to vacant ground.

The run was exciting and successful. About twenty fine buffalo were killed, and the choice pieces brought to camp, cooked and eaten amidst the merriment, mixed with something coarser, of the hunters. On this noisy rejoicing Mr. Parker looked with a sober aspect, and following the dictates of his religious feelings, he rebuked the Sabbath breakers quite severely. But for his influence among the men if he had not done so, or had not eaten so heartily of the tenderloin afterward, a circumstance which his irreverent critics did not fail to remark, to his prejudice; and upon the principle that the "partaker is as bad as the thief," they sat down on his lecture on Sabbath breaking as nothing better than pious humbug.

Dr. Marcus Whitman was another style of man. Whatever he thought of the wild ways of the mountain men he discreetly kept to himself, preferring to teach by example rather than precept, and showing no fastidious contempt for any kind of rough duty he might be called upon to perform. It was agreed between the two missionaries that Whitman should return to the States in search of more help, while Parker was to start for the Columbia river in search of a good site for their future mission.

In the meantime Rose was making preparations to claim the prize at the next rendezvous. The American Fur Company consisted of about half French and half Americans, and the contest for the prize was not so much an individual as a national one. It must not be supposed the trapper who won the prize of three hundred dollars would be the richer by that amount. The greater part of the money was spent in a large treat. If an American trapper won the prize, the treat was exclusively among the Americans, and if a French trapper won the prize it was the same among the French. At the end of the year, the trapper who had been so expert or lucky as to capture the most beaver would be considered the winning man, and from that time forward he would be assisted by his companions, in order to beat the best trapper of the other party.

The next day after the preaching the party started for the Tetons, from whence they intended to proceed to the headwaters of the Yellowstone. Bridger had informed them that up in the mountains in that region, there was a beautiful and extensive plain, and a large lake, and that on the streams running into and out of this lake there were plenty of Beaver.

The next morning, as they were riding up the banks of a small stream, they suddenly came upon a grove of choke-cherry bushes, loaded with ripe fruit. The trappers immediately surrounded the grove, about an acre in extent, and commenced eating the cherries, thinking them quite a treat. Now, it is well known, the grizzly bear is remarkably fond of choke-cherries, and scarcely had the trappers surrounded the grove and commenced eating, when there was a sudden rush through the bushes, a savage growl, and an immense grizzly made his appearance. A trapper by the name of

Caleb Wilkins, mounted on a mule, was near the spot where the grizzly emerged from the bushes, and the ferocious animal went for him at once. Caleb, seeing the bear advance, wheeled his mule and started; but the mule would not hurry, and the bear soon caught up with him, but it was evident the grizzly was a stranger to the habits of the mule, for as soon as he came within reach of that animal, he opened his ponderous jaws with the intention of grabbing him by the hinder parts; but the mule was on the alert, and as soon as the bear had come within reach, he let fly at him with his hind feet, nearly dislocating his jaw; but the bear, uttering a savage growl, continued the race, and again coming up with the mule, endeavored to seize him with his enormous paw. All this time the trappers were laughing and shouting: "Look out, Caleb!" "Go it, Caleb!" but finding the race was likely to end disastrously for Caleb and the mule, one of the trappers galloped up to the bear and shot him in the shoulder, and being wounded, the grizzly turned and started for the man who had fired the shot. Another and another shot was fired into the grizzly, and for some time he was kept busy wheeling and facing each new enemy, till at last a ball from one of the rifles struck him in a vital part, and he fell over and died. From that time forward the grizzly was known as "Caleb," and I believe he is called so to this day.

In journeying up the valley of the Yellowstone, the signs of volcanic disturbances were so noticeable that they gave rise to many quaint and curious remarks among the trappers. Sometimes they would come to a boiling spring, spouting the water many feet into the air. Again, they would see half a dozen of these boiling springs, all within the radius of an acre, and emitting a strong sulphurous smell. At one place they came upon a swamp, or rather an immense puddle of black mud, covering a space of four or five acres. This appeared to be all the time heaving, boiling and bubbling like a pot of mush, and several of the trappers shook their heads and remarked it was getting a little too close to the region of fire and brimstone to suit them, and that they would not be surprised to see a certain dark looking gentleman, with a cloven foot and a forked tail, start up and confront them at almost any moment.

On reaching the headwaters of the Yellowstone, they found it exactly as Bridger had described it. Away up in the mountains they found a large and beautiful lake, and plain covered with abundance of grass and beautiful flowers. The pasture was as green as though it was the spring instead of the fall of the year, and, although there was a slight frost almost every night, many choice and beautiful flowers could be seen in every direction. Beaver were also found to be plentiful on all the small streams in this region, and the boys now zealously commenced trapping, Rose never once forgetting his resolve to win the prize, sparing neither time nor labor to effect that object. He was careful in examining the haunts of the beaver, making use of all his knowledge and adroitness in setting his traps, and would often walk miles to find a good location, and so well did he succeed that he far outstripped his companions, and he was generally pronounced by his brother trappers to be the winning man.

CHAPTER XV.

IN WHICH ROSE GOES IT ALONE, LOSES HIS BEAVER SKINS, AND IS CHASED BY THE BLACKFEET.

Rose and his company continued to trap on the small streams near Yellowstone Lake, and were very successful, having succeeded in trapping a great many beaver.

Rose, still bent on winning the prize, would pack his traps and start for some distant stream, where he would often trap alone for days together,

and these solitary excursions proved very successful, and at the end of the first month he was
several skins ahead of any of his fellow trappers.

Finding that he met with more success away
from the main body, he persuaded Lewis and a
trapper named Howell, whom our readers will
remember as the unfortunate lover, to accompany
him to the dividing ridge of the eastern and
western slope, with the intention of trapping on
the tributaries of the Bitter Root and Jefferson
rivers. Here they found a paradise among the
mountains. Beautiful plains, interspersed with
small lakes and beaver ponds. The beaver on
these ponds did not appear to be at all shy, and it
seemed as if no trapper had ever before visited that
region. They could set on the banks of one of
these small lakes and see fifteen or twenty beaver
sporting about in the water. Suddenly, one of
them would bring his flat tail down upon the surface with a sound like the crack of a rifle, when
they would all instantly disappear; but only to
return in a few moments, and again go through
the same performance. Here the men went to
work with enthusiasm, and took a large number
of skins, and at the end of two weeks Rose found
he had come within one of catching as many as
the other two put together, and when they were

rejoined by Bridger and his company, Rose was found to be twenty-two skins ahead of any other man.

Having been informed by Bridger that in a few weeks the company would move down to Clark's Fork, where they would remain until they went into winter quarters, Rose tried to persuade Lewis and Howell to accompany him, in advance of the company. But this they would not agree to, Lewis declaring that he was not yet tired of his life, and that it would only be throwing it away to go down there so weak-handed.

Clark's Fork was supposed to be one of the most dangerous localities in the Rocky mountains. The stream ran through a part of the country lying between the Crows and the Blackfeet, and was often visited by both these nations, and as both the Crows and the Blackfeet were enemies to the white man, it was not at all prudent for them to visit this locality unless in full force. It was well known that their camp was even now continually watched by the Indians, who were hovering in the neighborhood, hoping to cut off some stray trapper, but Rose was not to be deterred by these danger signals. Knowing how much more successful he was when trapping by himself, and finding he could not persuade any of his companions to accompany him, he determined to go it alone. He was aware that if he left the camp in day time he would be seen and followed by Indians. He, therefore, one dark night, packed up his traps, saddled his horse, and with his trusty rifle on his shoulder, started at midnight for Clark's Fork.

It was a lonely, dark and hazardous journey, this midnight ride, through a wild and mountainous district, with nothing to guide him but the growth of willows and cotton wood that skirted the stream down which he was slowly wending his way. He could not leave the stream for any great distance, as he was compelled to keep the timber in view, and he was fearful of riding too close, lest he should be pounced upon by some lurking Indian or savage grizzly.

After riding an hour or so, Rose became more confident, and as his road now lay through a more open part of the country, he moved on much more rapidly than before.

On arriving at Clark's Fork, he kept himself concealed all through the day, and attended to his traps at early dawn, and in this way continued trapping for two weeks, and was successful, beyond his utmost expectations, for at the end of that time he had a roll of beaver skins as big around as his body. As the animals were getting a little shy he concluded to try his luck further down the stream, and not wishing to take his skins with him, there being between thirty and forty in number, he placed the roll in the hollow of a dead cottonwood tree, pushing them up as far as he could reach, then taking a pole he rammed them up seven or eight feet into the hollow, and thought that now they were perfectly safe, and packing up his traps he started that night several miles lower down the stream. Here he met with better luck than ever, having actually caught six beavers in one night, being one for every trap. Thinking it most likely that Bridger and his company had arrived at the upper end of Clark's Fork, and wishing to return to camp and astonish his companions with his fine lot of beaver skins, for Rose now felt assured that his late success had placed him so far ahead that no other trapper would attempt to compete with him, and with spirits light and buoyant, he packed his skins and traps, and started up stream for the dead cottonwood tree; but, alas! for the mutability of human events! On reaching the spot he found the tree had been torn down by grizzlies, and his beautiful pack of beaver skins had been torn into a thousand pieces by these ravenous animals, and the fur lay scattered around in every direction. This was a sad disappointment to Rose; but instead of discouraging him, it only made him the more determined to succeed, and he pushed on up the stream, with the expectation of joining his companions. As he was riding across a plain he came upon a dead buffalo, that had been lately shot. On examining the carcass he found that the brains had been taken out, and he knew at once it had been killed by Indians. A little father on he came to a second and third carcass, from which the brains had also been removed. He now felt certain the Indians were at no great distance. Wishing to ascertain their whereabouts, and to make sure he was not mistaken, he started across the prairie toward a mountain gap, or defile, which would take him to the bank of the Yellowstone. Passing through this gap he crossed a small plain about half a mile in width, reaching a bluff looking down into the Yellowstone. Here he saw a camp of about sixty or seventy Blackfeet. Rose tried o retreat without being seen, but it was too late; he had already been seen by the Indians, who now came yelling and swarming up the bluff. Rose headed his horse for the gap. Several of the Indians took along the ridge leading in the same direction, and as they had not more than half the distance to go, Rose saw that he was likely to be cut off, and again wheeling his horse he started down the plain. This prairie was covered with wild sage bushes, in many places growing ten feet high. The buffalo had made paths all through them. Rose followed some of those buffalo trails till he had placed four or five miles between himself and his pursuers, and as it was then about four o'clock in the afternoon, he determined to lay by till night before attempting to make his escape.

A little after midnight Rose again headed for the gap, and as he approached that narrow defile he began to feel a little nervous. If the Indians caught him in the gap, death was certain, and as he entered, he felt, to use a common expression, as if his heart was in his mouth, but, contrary to his expectations, he passed through in safety, and the next day he joined Bridger and his companions, who had, as he expected, just arrived at Clark's Fork. The boys were glad to see Rose, but instead of sympathizing with him they only laughed heartily at the joke the bears had played him.

On counting his skins he found he was still a considerable quantity ahead. The trappers, as we have before mentioned, are a little inclined to be superstitious. It appears that while Rose was trapping on the headwaters of the Jefferson he had caught a large white beaver. It had no spot or color about it; even its tail was perfectly white, and as this was a thing of very rare occurrence it was generally supposed by the trappers to be a fortunate omen, and that the lucky trapper would be successful in everything he undertook. Bridger, on hearing that a camp of Blackfeet were not far off, and knowing they were dangerous neighbors, determined to set out the next morning, with his company, and endeavor to make them leave that part of the country till the trapping season was over.

CHAPTER XVI.

IN WHICH HOWELL IS KILLED BY THE INDIANS. FIGHT WITH THE BLACKFEET. DEATH OF GODOIS.

Bridger was very much annoyed to find so large a band of hostile Indians in such close proximity to his camp. He was aware his men would be in constant danger; that, in fact, it would not be safe for any of them to go off trapping by themselves, as the savages were constantly on the alert.

A circumstance had occurred the day before Rose had joined his company, that determined Bridger to attack, and, if possible, drive the Blackfeet from the neighborhood.

Two trappers, Howell and Green, whose unfortunate love affairs, our readers will remember, had induced them to join the fur company, were trapping a few miles from camp, on the Yellowstone. As they were riding up the bank of the stream they saw six or eight Indians coming toward them. Wheeling their horses, with the intention of making for the camp, they saw another company of Indians below them; that, it fact, they were surrounded, and their only chance of escape was by the river. Forcing their horses down the steep bank, they plunged into the river and made for the opposite shore. Green slipped from the saddle and swam along beside his horse, while Howell kept his seat. The Indians commenced firing at them before they reached the opposite bank, and Howell received three shots in his back. With a groan he leaned forward on his horse, and his rifle fell from his hand into the river.

"Are you badly hurt?" inquired Green.

"I'm a dead man," exclaimed Howell, "and you had better leave me and do the best you can to save yourself."

But Green declared he would not leave him so long as there was any hope of saving him, and taking the wounded man's horse by the bridle, he forced the animals up the bank; then mounting his horse, and telling Howell to hold on with all his might, they started at full speed down the stream.

They were, however, on the wrong side of the river, and the Indians were between them and the camp, and were running down the stream with the intention of heading them off, but as their horses were good, Green and his companon were soon far enough ahead of the Indians to recross the river; but poor Howell was sinking fast, and passing through a miry place about a mile from camp, he fell off, and as Green could do him no good by staying with him, he hurried to camp in seach of assistance.

Some of the trappers returned with him at once, and Howell was brought into camp. His wounds proved mortal, and he died that night, thus terminating his unfortunate career.

Preparations were at once made to start for the Blackfeet camp in the morning, for their trapper blood was up, and they were determined to avenge the death of their companion.

There were about twenty Indian free trappers, who had attached themselves to Bridger's company, belonging to the Delaware and Shawnee tribes, and as they considered the Blackfeet their deadly foe, they were most anxious to join in the coming fray.

Two hours before the time appointed to start, the Indians were busy daubing themselves with war paint, which made them have a most hideous and ferocious appearance. They then went through with what they called the war dance, and declared themselves ready for the march, and Bridger, with about fifty of his men, started for the Yellowstone, the friendly Indians leading the way.

On arriving within sight of the Blackfeet camp, it was found they had ensconced themselves in a thick growth of cottonwood and willows, on the bank of the river, from which it seemed dangerous to attempt to move them; but the Delawares and Shawnees were not to be so easily balked of their prey. With rifle in one hand, and tomahawk in the other, they rushed into the thicket, yelling like demons, and the Blackfeet thinking, no doubt, the whole company of trappers had charged on them, rushed down the bank into the river and swam to an island in the middle of the stream, holding their guns out of the water with one hand to keep them dry. Here they fortified themselves behind a lot of drift timber, piling the logs around them so as to form a sort of fort. The trappers and friendly Indians took their position among the clumps of bushes along the banks of the stream.

It may appear strange to our readers, yet it is nevertheless true, that the feeling experienced by the trappers, when about to make a raid on a band of hostile Indians, resembles those of our country friends when going to visit a circus. It is relaxation from their usual employment, and a good time for fun, frolic and adventure is expected. Every trapper had selected a tree or clump of bushes, within fair rifle range of their enemies and whenever a Blackfoot exposed any part of his person, a ball from one of the trapper's rifle would send the unfortunate Indian to the happy hunting grounds. These fights may be considered a regular target practice. One of the Indians would hoist a breech-cloth above the logs, and in one minute it would be cut down by a bullet from one of the white men's rifles, followed by shouts and yells from the trapper who witnessed the shot; and, again, a trapper would place his wolfskin cap on his ramrod, and raise it above his place of concealment, and it would soon be perforated by an Indian bullet. In this way the fight went on for several hours, with but little advantage to either party.

Mark Head, who had taken his station behind a cottonwood stump, had, while loading his gun, stepped a little too much to one side, and received a slight wound in the fleshy part of his arm, and immediately called out, with his usual nasal drawl, "Boys, I'm shot!"

"What does he say?" inquired Lewis, who was lying behind a clump of bushes.

"He says he has shot one of the Indians," replied a trapper.

"No, I didn't, neither!" exclaimed Mark. "I said I was shot, myself." This was received with roars of laughter by his companions, who knew by his tone he was not seriously hurt.

One of the Delaware Indians swam his horse across the river to the foot of the island, and, dismounting, he crept up to within fifty yards of the fort, and climbing a large cottonwood tree, which overlooked their place of concealment, he fired three shots right in among them, killing an Indian at each shot, but the balls from the Blackfeet rifles were tearing the bark from the limb behind which he had concealed himself, and he was compelled to descend and beat a hasty retreat.

The fight continued till night, when the trappers returned to camp. The next morning they again visited the battle ground, but the Indians had departed, and Bridger was in hopes that, for a time at least, they had rid themselves of their troublesome neighbors.

Trapping now went on briskly, and for some

days no Indians, or Indian signs, could be seen, and the trappers again commenced to spread themselves out on the small streams within eight or ten miles of the camp, and Rose was still meeting with good success.

Two Frenchmen had for some time been trapping on a small stream running into the Yellowstone, and one of them, by the name of Godois, told Rose if he would accompany him the next morning he would show him where there was lots of beaver and accordingly, the next day, after visiting his traps, he mounted his horse, and in company with the Frenchman (Godois), started to examine the stream, about four miles distant from camp.

Rose rode along the bluff, while Godois rode up the stream for the purpose of looking after his traps. Rose, although he could not see his companion, could hear him quite plainly, he being not more than one hundred yards distant. Godois, as he came upon each of his traps would call out and inform Rose of his success. The first trap was a "cut-foot." On examining the second trap he called out, "a beaver." The third trap was "sprung." At the fourth trap he called out, "another beaver." This was the last trap he ever examined. Scarcely had he uttered the last words when Rose heard the crack of a half dozen fusees. He heard Godois call out, "Oh!" and he knew that his companion had been shot by Indians. As he wheeled his horse to return to camp, he saw that half a dozen of the savages were heading in that direction to cut him off, and again wheeling his horse, he galloped up stream, and making a long detour, arrived safely in camp.

Some of the trappers accompanied him the next day, and found poor Godois lying dead, with his face in the water, his body pierced by a number of arrows and bullets. The Indians had taken his rifle, shot bags, traps and horse. They buried poor Godois on the bank of the stream, and returned to camp.

CHAPTER XVII.

IN WHICH ROSE STRIKES A BONANZA—WINTER QUARTERS—FLIGHT OF CHILSIPEE.

The death of the two trappers, Howell and Godois, caused the trappers to be a little more cautious in their solitary excursions, and for some time they were compelled to trap in squads, much to the annoyance of our friend Rose, who was certainly more successful when trapping alone.

Meek, Crow, and two other trappers, had visited

the stream where Godois was killed, but finding the Blackfeet a little too thick in that vicinity, they were compelled to leave in a hurry. They reported beaver to be very plentiful in that region, and Rose, who was very anxious to make up for the skins he had lost by the grizzlies, determined to visit the stream and try his luck at all hazards. Accordingly, one clear, frosty night, in the latter part of October, just after dark, he packed his traps, mounted his horse, and started for the dangerous trapping grounds. On reaching the stream he rode his horse into a small hollow, where grass was plentiful, and where he could not be seen by any one passing up or down the stream. Shouldering his traps, he started up the bed of the stream, moving along cautiously and noiselessly, with both eye and ear on the alert to catch the slightest sound. In this way a mile was passed over. His traps were properly and carefully set, and Rose returned to his horse, which he found quite safe, and crawling into a thicket of bushes, and rolling himself in his blanket, was soon sound asleep. About daylight he awoke and started up the stream to visit his traps, and again met with his usual success. Three beaver and a "kitten" were the fruits of the night's trapping. After skinning the animals Rose crawled into a growth of heavy willows, and again laid himself down.

Just as the western sun was gilding the tops of the western hills Rose awoke, and creeping cautiously to the edge of the grove he looked carefully around. Everything appeared to be quiet. About fifty yards up the stream was a small knoll on which stood a large cottonwood tree, and Rose was aware that from this spot he could see a long distance both up and down the stream, and as the cottonwood would be a good shelter he thought he would take up his station there. Just as he was about to start, he thought he saw something moving at the foot of the tree, and on a close inspection discovered it to be the head of an Indian, peering around the trunk. Rose drew a little farther back into the bushes, and watched the movements of his red neighbor with a great deal of interest. He was a Blackfoot, and after looking around the tree for some time, he arose to his feet, and gazed earnestly down the stream. Not being satisfied with this scenting, he clambered up into the tree, where he remained about fifteen minutes, noticing closely every grove or clump of bushes as far as his eye could reach down the stream. Seeming to be at length satisfied that no dangerous visitors were around, he descended and gave three sharp whistles, like the call of some wild bird, which was answered by some one away up the stream, and four Indians made their appearance from that direction and joined their companion under the cottonwood tree. One of the Indians had half a dozen beaver skins with him, which they proceeded at once to stretch and pin to the ground to dry.

After conversing for some little time, one of them again climbed the tree, and after a long and careful survey, descended, apparently quite satisfied, and the four Indians again started up the stream, as Rose thought, with the intention of visiting some more of their traps. This appeared to have been the case, as in about an hour they returned with three more beaver skins, which they likewise stretched. In about an hour Rose could tell, by the way they examined their fire-arms, they were about to start out on some expedition, most likely to hunt as they moved off toward the hills, still leaving their companion on guard beneath the tree.

Instead of Rose thinking this a good opportunity to make his escape, he was inwardly calculating how to get possession of the beaver skins, and after the Indians had been gone about half an hour he concluded it was about time to make the attempt.

He had two or three times drawn a bead on the Indian, and as often lowered his weapon, not that he felt any compunction of conscience at killing a Blackfoot; he only hesitated because he thought the other Indians were not far enough away, and might hear the crack of his rifle.

Just, however, as he had made up his mind to put an end to the Blackfoot, he heard the report of two fusees in the direction the Indians had gone. The Blackfoot beneath the tree sprang to his feet, and, after taking a careful survey, started in a lope after his companions.

Rose waited a few minutes, then crept carefully toward the knoll, seized and rolled up the nine beaver skins belonging to the Indians, and hurried down the stream in the direction of his horse, and the trappers were astonished that evening to see Rose ride into camp with twelve beaver and a "kitten" skin, and were much amused as he related his adventure.

The company continued on Clark's Fork for some little time, but as the cold weather was fast setting in, Bridger began to think it was high time to find a suitable location for winter quarters. The camp accordingly moved down onto the Yellowstone, and at length found an excellent situation near the mouth of the Big Horn.

Their camp was at the foot of a high hill, from the top of which the country could be seen for fifty or sixty miles in every direction. A small fort was built on the summit, and one or two men were always stationed there with a spy glass to keep a lookout, and notify their companions of any coming danger. Just below the camp was a large growth of cottonwood, sufficient to supply their animals with food all through the coming winter. Cottonwood bark is considered excellent food for horses, and as long as sufficiency of this can be obtained, the animals keep in good order. Each trapper is compelled to skin enough bark each day for two horses, and so expert were they in barking the limbs, that it took them but a short time to get the required quantity.

So well trained were the horses and mules belonging to the trappers, that when grazing, perhaps a mile or two from camp, if they heard the yell of a band of Indians or even if the white men would commence yelling, the animals would break for camp at the top of their speed.

The place where the camp was situated was in the heart of the Blackfeet country, and Chilsipee recognized at once her old camping ground, and from the top of the hill could point out the direction of her native village, about fifty miles distant. She also pointed out the places where her nation had fought the Crows.

For some days she had seemed more than usually excited, and one day as she was looking from the old fort toward her native hills, Rose asked her if she would not like to go back and see her people. She did not answer, but he could see the big tears well up into her eyes, and he knew she was thinking of home.

A few mornings after this it was discovered that Chilsipee had disappeared. She had packed up and taken everything belonging to her, and she had also taken one of the company's very best horses. It was generally supposed she had been assisted in her flight by either an Indian or a white man, or she could not possibly have eluded the vigilance of the guard. But, be that as it may, that was the last the trappers ever heard of their pet, Chilsipee.

Although the trappers had constructed their lodges, and made every preparation for the coming winter, they had not altogether quit trapping. The weather was remarkably fine for the beginning of winter, and many of the trappers continued their occupation, and Rose had taken one or two more solitary excursions, in which, although he met with his usual success, there was no adventure worth relating.

At length winter set in in reality. Trapping was over for the season, and the men settled down to the usual routine of winter quarters.

CHAPTER XVIII.

IN WHICH ROSE AND HIS COMPANIONS HAVE A SKIRMISH WITH THE BLACKFEET—MANHEAD KILLED — HUNTING EXCURSION — ROSE WOUNDED.

The winter of 1835 and '36 proved to be a severe one; the streams were all frozen over to a great depth, and mountain and plain were covered with a thick coating of snow, and the trappers had now nothing to do but strip cottonwood bark for their horses, go on an occasional hunting excursion, play cards or dominoes, and tell long and marvelous tales of "narrow and hairbreadth escapes by flood and field;" but no matter how cold and stormy the weather a constant watch was always kept at the little fort on the hill near the camp.

One afternoon in the latter part of January, one of the guards came down from the little fort and informed the company that a band of Blackfeet had stopped on the opposite side of the river, about four miles below; that there were thirty-seven of them, and that it was evidently their intention to camp there for the night. Bridger determined to get rid of these troublesome neighbors at once, and next morning started down the river with a company of about fifty trappers, including some Delawares and Flatheads, who, as usual, were painted up for the occasion.

On arriving near the Blackfoot camp it was discovered the Indians had not been idle, but had. during the night, constructed a sort of fort. They had shown a great deal of sagacity in selecting their location, as there were no trees or bushes within rifle shot, behind which the trappers could shelter themselves, and it would be laboring under great disadvantage in attacking the Blackfeet under such circumstances. They, therefore, contented themselves by riding around the fort and trying a few shots at long range. Rose, and a Delaware Indian by the name of Manhead, had ridden around to the back of the fort, which had not been as well constructed as the other portion of it, and alighting from their horses, they approached as near as they could with safety. They then commenced rolling forward a huge snowball, behind which they sheltered themselves, and in this manner contrived to get near enough to do some execution; but the balance of the trappers, finding they could do nothing with the Blackfeet while in that fortified position, started back to camp in squads of two or three at a time, until Rose and the Delaware were the only ones left. Finding they were deserted, Rose and his companion remounted their horses, and started to recross the slough, but the Blackfeet, finding how matters stood, rushed out of the fort in hot pursuit. On reaching the opposite side of the slough, unfortunately, Rose and his companion struck a high bank, which the horses seemed incapable of surmounting. Getting off their horses, they contrived, by yells and blows, to make them scramble to the top, but the savages were now within gun shot, and just as they remounted Manhead received a wound in the calf of his leg, the ball passing upward to the knee. Urging forward their horses, they were soon out of range of the Blackfoot guns and arrows, when Manhead exclaimed, "Rose, I'm a dead man; I am wounded with a poisoned ball!" This proved to be the case, for scarcely had they reached camp, when the Delaware's leg swelled to an enormous size, and he died in a few hours in great agony.

Perhaps our readers may not be aware of the method resorted to by the Indians to poison their bullets. It is done in this way: A small piece of buffalo meat is placed on the end of a forked stick, and a rattlesnake is induced to strike his fangs into it. This poisoned meat is then dried, pounded up into powder and placed in a small bag. When the Indian intends to use one of these poisoned bullets, he first puts it in his mouth and chews it for some time, then dips it into the bag, and the slighest wounds from one of these bullets will cause death.

The next morning after the fight the trappers again started down the river, determined to put the Indians to flight at all hazards; but on arriving at the Indian fort they found it deserted, and, destroying the fort, they again returned to camp. Game was getting very scarce. Continued hunting in the neighborhood had driven away the buffalo, and the trappers found it necessary to go farther afield; and this was by no means a healthy undertaking. Bands of Blackfeet were known to be prowling around in the vicinity, and a hunt at any great distance from camp was not likely to be conducive to longevity; but the trappers, although resting from their usual occupation, found that their stomachs and appetites were as much on the alert as ever, and that consequently, meat must be had. Accordingly, on the second day of February, (that being the date as nearly as they could calculate it,) four of the trappers, viz: Rose, Joe

Meek, Jack Larrison, and Mark Head, started on a hunting expedition, Clark's Fork being selected as the best place to find buffalo. On account of the deep snow around the upper valley of Clark's Fork, the buffalo were snowed in. They took with them seven or eight pack horses and mules. They met with tolerable success during the day, and contrived to load four of their animals. At night they halted in a thicket, on the banks of Clark's Fork, and, not daring to kindle a fire, they secured their animals, rolled themselves in their buffalo skins or blankets, and, although the night was bitter cold, they slept till daylight in the morning.

During the night Rose dreamed a peculiar dream, and, although he was not superstitious, the dream seemed to impress itself forcibly on his imagination, so much so that he could not get it out of his head. He dreamed he met a huge grizzly. "Caleb," as the trappers called him, was standing upright on his hind legs, and insisted on shaking hands with Rose, who offered him his left hand. This "Caleb" refused to take, making signs that the shaking must be done with the right. Rose accordingly stretched out his right and gave "Caleb's" paw a hearty shake.

The next morning Rose told his dream to his

companions. Meek shook his head and exclaimed:
(See "The River of the West," written by Mrs.
Francis Fuller Victor, page 172.)

"You had better look out, Rose, or you'll shake
hands with Beelzebub before night." Beelzebub
was a nickname for the Blackfeet.

After the trappers had fed and packed their
animals they started toward the camp, hoping to
find more game as they went along. Rose, who
was an excellent shot, did most of the shooting,
while the other three men skinned, cut up the
meat and packed the animals. Several buffalo
were seen, but they were so wild that a hunter
could not get near enough for a shot. Rose told
his companions he was certain there were Indians
not far off.

The country through which they were riding
was hilly. Rose was, as usual, leading the way,
followed by the pack horses, the three trappers
bringing up the rear. Just ahead of them was a
small ravine. On approaching within about ten
feet of it, eight or nine Indians suddenly sprang
up and confronted him with the customary "Ho,
ho." As quick as a flash Rose wheeled his horse,
while at the same time six or seven guns were discharged at him. The Indians had scared Rose's
horse, and he thinks his rearing and plunging

saved his life. One of the balls passed through his cap, another slightly wounded him across the breast, cutting the strings of his shot pouch, which fell to the ground. One ball passed through his buckskin glove, slightly wounding his wrist. But his worst wound was a ball that passed through the right elbow, entering the back of the arm just below the joint, and passing out at the forepart of the arm. The Indians then rushed forward with the intention of seizing the horse by the bridle, and one of them was close enough to place his hand on Rose's knee, while he reached for the bridle with the other. Rose struck the savage a blow in the face with his riding whip, and his horse springing forward at the same time, carried him beyond the Indian's reach. His rifle, however, fell to the ground, he not being able to hold it with his disabled arm.

Rose, when hunting, always carried his rifle in a buckskin cover, and this proved a fortunate thing for him, as he was fully thirty yards away before they had taken it out from its buckskin case. Then, however, a ball whistled past his ear, and he heard the well known crack of his own rifle. Looking back he saw fifty or sixty more Indians pouring down out of the cedars and coming at full speed.

The trappers, with their pack horses, were in full retreat, galloping for their lives. The pack on one of the mules turned, and, Larrison seeing it, cut it loose with his hunting knife, and let it go, at the same time calling out to Rose: "Are you killed, old boy?"

"Not killed," replied Rose, "but badly wounded. Hurry forward, boys, and save yourselves, if you can."

Rose and his companions got back safe to camp, he being more dead than alive. His broken arm grating and swinging, for a long thirty mile ride.

CHAPTER XIX.

IN WHICH MASELINO IS WOUNDED—THE BLACK-FEET BENT ON EXTERMINATION—BRIDGER BUILDS A FORT.

Rose's wound proved more serious than was at first supposed. It was carefully examined by the Indian medicine man and Bridger, who were both of the opinion that he had been wounded by a poisoned ball, and it was only the great loss of blood that prevented it from at once proving fatal. As it was, he was fearfully prostrated, and for some days his life was despaired of. His arm swelled to an enormous size, and the skin peeled off to his shoulder; his nervous system was fearfully disorganized. The loss of blood, and the poison of the bullet, had occasioned such nervous irritability that he could not bear the least noise or motion. If a gun was discharged in camp it would nearly throw him into convulsions. His mess-mates, Lewis and Crow, did all in their power to alleviate his sufferings, Crow, especially, proving an excellent nurse. In about a week the wound assumed a more favorable appearance, and for the first time hopes were entertained of his recovery.

One morning, about a week or ten days after Rose had received his wound, one of the guards came down from the little fort on the hill, and informed the trappers that a large band of Blackfeet were camping about four miles below, on the Yellowstone, and that they were putting up their lodges, as though they intended to stay.

One or two mornings after this, Maselino started up toward the little fort, with the intention of reconnoitering. From some cause the fort had not been occupied by the trappers the night before, and as the Mexican approached to within fifty yards, he was fired upon by two Indians, who had contrived to gain possession of it. One of the balls hit Maselino on the ankle, breaking it, and he fell to the ground. The Indians, thinking they had a sure thing of their victim, rushed out of the fort with the intention of finishing him. Maselino was not to be so easily caught. The hill was steep and covered with snow, and, notwithstanding his broken ankle, rolled himself up like a ball, and actually rolled down the hill, into camp, where his wound was attended to, and some of the trappers, rushing up the hill, soon dislodged the Indians.

The next day the Blackfeet Indians were joined by two more large bands, and for several days large bodies of Indians continued to arrive, till the Blackfeet camp consisted of nearly a thousand lodges, and fifteen or sixteen hundred warriors.

In the meantime, Bridger had not been idle. It was evident the Indians intended mischief; in fact, that they meant nothing less than extermination, and preparations were at once made to receive them. About one acre of ground was marked off, and strong forks were driven into the ground at short distances apart. In these, heavy poles were laid. The trappers then went to cutting logs, none of them less than a foot through. One end was sunk in the snow, and placed in an upright position against the poles. The logs were about eight feet high, and were as close together as they could be put, leaving only an occasional space large enough for the barrel of a rifle. In the centre of the inclosure a block-house was erected, in which were placed the traps, and all the property belonging to the trappers, together with the wounded men and squaws. The block-house and palisade were finished in what may seem an incredible short space of time; trappers, Indians and squaws all working with a will, for they knew they were working for their lives.

Bridger had among his property, one hundred and fifty or two hundred guns. These were all loaded, so that when the trappers had discharged their rifles, they could, if necessary, blaze away with the trade guns, witnout stopping to reload.

Scarcely were their preparations completed, when the lookout perceived that something was going on at the Indian camp, and at night a Delaware scout came in and informed them that the attack would be made the next morning, as the Blackfeet were mixing their war paints, and some of them had already painted themselves.

In the meantime, Rose was still lying feeble and helpless. Circumstances that were going on around the camp were not calculated to allay his nervous irritability. The great object for which he had labored so long and so diligently, and for which he had undergone so many hardships and privations, and often risked even life itself, was about to slip from his grasp when success was almost certain. What rendered the matter still worse was that if Rose did not gain the trapper's prize, the next man on the list was a Frenchman by the name of Shonare, and if the prize was awarded to him the Americans would get none of the treat, or receive any benefit from it. The thought that this might be the case, was a constant source of annoyance and irritation to Rose. And this was not all. A fearful struggle was about to take place, to which the bravest and most reckless of the trappers looked forward with no pleasant anticipation, and as Rose was always one of the foremost in affairs of this kind, he felt miserable that he could not make one in the coming fray. Bridger resolved to keep the Indians on the outside of the palisade, if possible; but if they should be stormed and carried, the trappers resolved, as a last resort, to retire to the block-house, and fight to the last man.

Early in the morning, the Delawares and Flatheads commenced making preparations to receive the enemy, and were thoroughly daubed with red and black paint, when the lookout from the little fort gave notice that the Blackfeet were formed into solid columns on the ice, and commenced their march up the river toward the trappers' camp. They were armed with rifles, fusees or trade guns, bows and arrows, and spears, and in their war paint and feathers, made a most formidable appearance. As soon as they came within three hundred yards, the Delawares and Flatheads left the fort and started down to meet them, screeching and yelling with all their might, and took their station behind bushes and trees, threatening to give their enemies a warm reception as soon as they came within range.

From the high banks of the river the trappers' fort could now be plainly seen, and the Blackfeet came to a halt, and remained there for nearly half an hour, evidently holding a pow-wow, or deliberation. They felt certain that if they attacked the trappers' fort, the slaughter among their men would be tremendous, and after counting the cost, they seemed to have come to the conclusion that it would not pay, and accordingly faced about and returned to their camp.

A day or two after, the Indians began to leave, several of their bands going toward their village on the Musselshell river, and others scattering in different directions, it being impossible for so large a body of Indians to remain together, on account of the difficulty in procuring provisions.

After the departure of the Indians, everything went on as usual in the trappers' camp, and several hunting excursions were inaugurated, the white men generally going in pretty good force, as roving bands of Indians were known to be in the vicinity.

There was in the camp, a tall, green, lanky fellow, who was always known by the name of "Cotton." He received this nick-name on account of his hair being nearly white. He was an easy, good natured fellow, and had been camp-keeper since the last rendezvous. One day he got permission to accompany a hunting party, and had borrowed an old, bob-tailed horse for the occasion. As they were returning to camp with their game they were chased by a band of Indians, and as "Cotton" could not get his old horse out of a jog-trot, it was evident he must be overtaken. As the trappers passed him he called out:

"Boys, tell Bridger poor old 'Cotton's' a goner!" The trappers, however, would not allow this, and facing about they kept the Indians in check till "Cotton" was out of danger.

CHAPTER XX.

IN WHICH ROSE IS ASSISTED BY HIS BROTHER TRAPPERS. THE RENDEZVOUS—THE DUEL.

As spring approached, Rose's wounded arm began slowly, but surely, to mend, but when the company left their winter quarters and started up the Big Horn river to begin their spring campaign among the beaver, Rose was not sufficiently recovered to attend to his traps. This was a great source of annoyance and vexation to him. The Frenchman, Shonare, was exerting himself to the utmost to catch up with Rose, and his brother trappers would often say:

"Come, Rose, old fellow, you must hurry up that arm of yours, or the Frenchman will beat us!" This Rose determined he should not do, and in the beginning of May, with his fusee in his belt, he loaded up his traps, mounted his horse, and with his arm still in a sling, started off with the rest of the trappers. Lewis, Meek and Kit Carson were now determined Rose should win the prize, and they, together with other trappers, assisted him in setting his traps, Rose always pointing out the spot where he wished them to be set, and his luck, or success, or whatever you may be pleased to call it, was astonishing, and he soon began to leave the Frenchman far behind.

Rose says he was very fortunate in trapping that spring, but he also acknowledges that his brother trappers were continually throwing in a beaver or two, so as to make sure of beating his rival, Shonare.

The company were now trapping on Powder river, and beaver were quite plenty, and trapping was carried on more peaceably than it had been for some time, the Indians appearing to have a wholesome dread of Bridger's company. Anyhow, they were not molested by them during the spring hunt.

Nothing extraordinary occurred until the company moved up among some of the small streams, near the foot of Wind river mountain. Some of the trappers who were out hunting, saw three large bears. These animals, as soon as they saw the trappers, attempted to get away from them. The trappers followed, yelling with all their might. One of the largest bears started in the direction of the camp. Several of the Indian women were seated under a tree embroidering moccasins, as the grizzly, scared at the yells of the pursuing trappers, rushed among them, scattering them in every direction. His pursuers soon caught up with him, however, and a few shots put an end to the hunt.

At length the time for the rendezvous was

drawing near, and Bridger and his company prepared to start for Green river, where, as usual, it
was to be held. They were well satisfied with
their spring hunt, having taken a great many
beaver skins, and Rose, although still compelled
to keep his arm in a sling, felt quite confident of
being able to gain the prize. One thing, however,
made them feel rather uneasy. Shonare, instead of
accompanying the trappers to Green river, had,
with one of his companions, stayed behind, with
the intention of trapping as long as possible,
hoping by some good streak of fortune, to catch
up with or beat Rose, and Bridger and his company had been at the rendezvous two weeks before
he made his appearance. The Frenchman, however,
had not been very successful. They had lost several
of their traps and brought in but very few skins,
and when the books of the company were posted
up it was announced that Rose was the winner, he
having been credited with forty-one skins more
than any other trapper. This news was received
by the Americans with great rejoicing, and cheer
after cheer rent the air, while the Frenchmen in
their turn were much crest-fallen, and Shonare,
especially, was exasperated to such a degree that he
mounted his horse, and riding backward and
forward among the trappers, he called out in a
loud voice:

"The Americans are no men! The Americans are children! and I can beat them with switches!"

Shonare was a powerful man, and as he rode backward and forward, with the butt of his gun resting on his knee, he looked around defiantly, as though daring any of the Americans to take it up. Kit Carson, who had heard the Frenchman bragging, stepped into his lodge and took down a couple of large pistols. They were each about a foot and a half long, and known among the trappers as "horse pistols." These he carefully loaded, and placing one of them in his belt he mounted his horse.

Some of his companions, who saw the smile on his countenance, asked him what he was going to do, it having been a noticeable fact that whenever Kit was about to enter into some deadly affray his face always wore a peculiar smile, as though he was about to perpetrate some excellent joke. Without stopping to answer any questions, Kit rode close alongside of Shonare, who was still threatening the Americans with switches. He drew his pistols and called out:

"Shonare, prepare to defend yourself!" The two men then turned their horses and faced each other, and two reports were heard, almost simultaneously. Shonare had raised his gun to his shoulder and discharged it without taking good aim, as his ball only knocked off Kit Carson's cap, without doing him any other injury, while Kit's shot broke Shonare's right arm in two places. The Frenchmen immediately gathered around their companion and carried him to his tent, while Kit called out:

"Hold on, Shonare, I'll give you another shot, if you're not satisfied!" but the Frenchman, if not satisfied, certainly had enough of it, and begged his companions not to let Kit Carson come near him, while Kit returned to his lodge, smiling all over his face, as though the whole thing was an excellent joke. (See Life of Kit Carson, page 92.)

The goods from St. Louis having arrived at the rendezvous, the long expected treat was in order, and Rose purchased five gallons of alcohol at thirty-two dollars a gallon. This, together with the sugar that was required to make it palatable, cost Rose one hundred and seventy-five dollars, leaving him a balance of one hundred and twenty-five dollars of his prize money.

It must not be supposed that with this amount of liquor the trappers commenced a drunken debauch. Nothing of the sort. Several of the trappers were temperate and would not touch it at all, while the others, without getting intoxicated, had a merry, jovial time for four or five days. Another grand treat was also indulged in at this time by the company. Flour was a dollar a pint, and each of the trappers would throw in that amount. The flour was then placed in the camp-kettle, made up into paste with water, and baked in cakes on the coals. This, however, was an expensive luxury that the boys did not often indulge in.

While Bridger's company were at the rendezvous they were joined by an Indian whom they called "Little Blackfoot." He was small but well made, and had rather a romantic history. He had, while in his own tribe, fallen in love with the chief's daughter, but the chief refusing to give his consent to their union, the young couple had followed the example of their more civilized neighbors, by running off and joining the Flatheads, with whom they lived as man and wife. Little Blackfoot was the best runner in his nation, and his speed was astonishing. He would run around all day with a party of hunters, they being on horseback, and kill as many buffalo as any of them, and return at night fresh as a daisy. Lewis, Rose and Kit Carson, who considered themselves good runners, tried their speed with Little Blackfoot, but neither in long or short distances could they compete with him, and they all pronounced him the best runner they had ever seen.

In the course of our narrative we shall refer to Little Blackfoot again.

––––––

CHAPTER XXI.

IN WHICH THERE ARE FRESH ARRIVALS AT THE REN-
DEZVOUS—LEWIS AND SUBORAH TAKEN PRISONERS
BY THE SIOUX—DEATH OF SUBORAH, AND ES-
CAPE OF LEWIS—THE TRAPPER'S TRICK.

Among the fresh arrivals at the rendezvous from St. Louis, were two white ladies, and as these were the first who had ever penetrated that remote region, they were looked upon, both by trappers and Indians, with astonishment, veneration and awe. They reminded the trappers of their mothers and sisters, and the girls they had left behind them, and the Indians looked upon them as beings of an-other and higher sphere.

Not only did the trappers gaze upon the new-comers with admiration, but united to this startling effect of memory, was respect for religious devotion which had inspired them to undertake the long and dangerous journey to the Rocky mountains, and also a sentiment of pity for what they knew only too well, yet remained to be encountered by those delicate women in the prosecution of their duty.

Mrs. Whitman was a large, stately, fair skinned woman, with blue eyes and light, auburn, almost golden hair. Her manners were at once dignified and gracious. She was, both by nature and education, a lady, and had a lady's appreciation of all that was courageous and refined; yet not without an element of romance and heroism in her disposition strong enough to have impelled her to undertake a missionary's life in the wilderness.

Mrs. Spalding, the other lady, was more delicate than her companion, yet equally earnest and zealous in the cause she had undertaken. The Indians would turn their gaze from the dark haired, dark eyed Mrs. Spalding, to what was, to them, more interesting, golden hair and blue eyes of Mrs. Whitman, and they seemed to regard them both as beings of a superior nature.

Dr. Whitman and his lady would listen for hours to the tales of adventure as told by the trappers; their battles with the Blackfeet; their buffalo hunts, and their encounters with the grizzly bears. If the reverend gentleman and lady could only have foreseen what was before them, the tragic and bloody end to their missionary labors, they would have returned to St. Louis without a moment's delay. (See Chapter xxxiii.)

Kit Carson had once resided in Taos, a thriving town in New Mexico, and as recollections of that place were of so pleasing a nature, he would often speak of it in the most enthusiastic manner, making it out to be almost a paradise. He would describe its wealth, its beautiful Senorettas, and its lively dances and fandangos; and his description had such an effect on the imagination of some of the trappers, that they agreed to leave the fur company and accompany him to that place. And, accordingly, a few days before the rendezvous broke up, Kit Carson, Joe Lewis, Jack Robinson, and a Frenchman by the name of Suborah, started on foot for Taos.

Previous to their departure they had settled up with the company, sold their horses, and Carson and Suborah had disposed of their wives, as they were not willing to take an Indian wife among the Mexican Senoras. Carson appeared sorry to part from his wife. He had purchased her when a young girl from the Snake Diggers. These are considered more intelligent than the Humboldt Diggers. Kit's wife, for whom he had given a horse, was a small, good looking squaw, quick and intelligent, and in a short time spoke the American language fluently. But Kit had made up his mind to go to Taos and did not wish to be burdened with a squaw wife. Rose was sorry to part from his friend Lewis. They had been raised together, had come to the mountains together, and seemed more like brothers than friends. But Lewis was determined to accompany Kit, and accordingly one morning, after a hearty hand-shaking, they started for New Mexico.

Nothing of interest occurred during the first few days of their journey until they reached the mountains of Colorado. As they came to that portion of the uplands, not far from where Leadville now stands, they found it necessary to cross a stream, along the banks of which was a thick growth of willows and cottonwood. Lewis and Suborah were about two hundred yards in advance of the others, and walking along close to the bushes, looking for a good place to cross, when they were surprised by a band of about thirty Sioux Indians. Carson and Robinson, who were on the side of the hill, immediately turned and fled. They were good runners, and contrived to make their escape. The Indians at once disarmed Lewis and his companion, taking from them both their rifles and knives. One of the chiefs wishing to test the quality of the rifle, pointed it at Suborah and shot him through the body, while a second Indian at once proceeded to scalp him. Lewis, seeing it would be his turn next, wheeled suddenly around, knocked down an Indian who stood beside him and dashed into the bushes and reached the stream, into which he plunged, and diving beneath the water contrived to reach some bushes on the other side before he raised his head. He then saw the Indians rushing up and down the stream in search of him, looking into every thicket of bushes, and plunging their spears into the water along the bank. Fortunately they had no conception he had crossed the stream. He remained in his hiding place till night; then, without arms of any description, and minus his hat, he started for Fort Laramie.

He traveled mostly by night for fear of encountering Indians, and in about four days he reached the Fort, nearly starved to death, and his moccasins completely worn out.

After recruiting for some days at Laramie, he started for St. Louis, and soon got a situation in a surveying party.

Carson and Robinson returned to the fur company and reported Lewis and Suborah both killed by the Indians, and Rose never knew but that was the case till two years after, when he returned to St. Louis.

The company were making for the Tetons, when they were joined by Carson and Robinson. Trappers now commenced in all eagerness, and Bridger was going to try once more the head waters of Snake River.

Among the new comers who had joined the party was an Irishman by the name of Dick Williams, and a man by the name of Ward; the latter was bald headed and was nick-named "Figure-head" by the trappers. These two men, being fresh comers, were of course made camp keepers, and for some time they seemed quite satisfied with their position; but at last the Irishman began to grumble. He said it was a thunderin' shame, so it was, that himself and "Figure-head" (they were camp keepers in Rose's lodge,) should be compelled to stay in the camp, cooking, like a parcel of women, while the boys were out huntin', trappin' and enjoyin' themselves.

"Faith, boys," said Dick, "couldn't yees let meself an' 'Figure-head' try it for once?" Rose, Carson, and his other mess mates determined to let the greenies try it, and concocted a plan to give them a good scare. They were allowed to accompany Rose the next day on a hunt. They met with poor success till just before night, when Rose killed a buffalo. The animal was at once skinned and the usual portion packed on the horses. It was now getting dark, and before reaching camp they had to pass through a deep canyon. By pre-concerted plans, some of the trappers were hid behind rocks, and as the party passed they shot off their guns. Rose pretended to fall from his horse, and the camp keepers started for the camp at the top of their speed, and declared that they had been attacked by a hundred Indians, and that poor Rose had been riddled with bullets.

You can fancy their astonishment at seeing Rose the next morning, as well as ever.

CHAPTER XXII.

IN WHICH THE BLACKFEET ATTEMPT A RUSE— MARK HEAD ATTACKED BY A GRIZZLY.

Bridger and his company continued trapping on the head waters of the Green river for some time, meeting with pretty good success. Occasionally they would cross over to the tributaries of Snake river, beaver being quite plentiful on some of the small mountain streams.

One morning, just after the trappers had returned to camp, they having been out examining their camp, a gun was heard in the hills close by. The guards immediately gave the yell, and horses and mules started at full speed for camp. The trappers, rifle in hand, rushed out of their lodges to ascertain what was going on. In the distance a solitary Indian was seen coming down the hill in the direction of the camp, carrying a large and beautiful flag. He was discovered to be a Blackfoot, and some of the trappers were for shooting him at once, but Bridger ordered them not to injure him. The Blackfoot marched boldly into camp. He informed Bridger he had procured the flag from the Hudson Bay Company, with whom his people had been in the habit of trading. He said the rest of his band were in the hills and wished to hold a "pow-wow" with the white chief, meaning Bridger; that they had a large quantity of beaver skins to trade, and wanted in return blankets, powder, knives, etc. Then waving his flag, thirty-six Black-feet Indians made their appearance and marched boldly into camp. They told Bridger that their skins were at their camp, or village, about fifteen miles distant, and they seemed to be on the most friendly terms.

The Delawares, Flatheads, and Nez Perces belonging to Bridger's company, looked on the new comers with suspicion and distrust, and seemed only to wait an opportunity to pitch into their mortal enemies, and several of the white trappers told Bridger he had better kill every mother's son of them or he would be very apt to rue it. Little Blackfoot, the runner, said the Blackfeet were lying, and that their coming into the white man's camp was only a trick to stampede the horses or try and murder some of the trappers. But Bridger would listen to none of them. He thought the story about their beaver skins might possibly be true, and that it would not do to lose the chance of making a profitable trade. Nevertheless, he cautioned them to keep a sharp lookout, and not allow them an opportunity to take any advantage.

The Blackfeet made themselves quite at home. They danced their war dance, showed the white men how they painted their horses when preparing to go on the war-path, and when, in the afternoon, a herd of buffalo made their appearance, they assisted the trappers in killing some of them and bringing the meat into camp. That night the Blackfeet left, as they said, for their village, where the trappers were to meet them the next day, and Bridger made the chief a present of a blanket and a calico shirt with which he seemed much pleased.

The next morning the trappers broke camp and started for the stream where they were to meet the Blackfeet, but no Indians were there. They found the carcasses of one or two buffalo that had been killed that morning, but the Blackfeet had disappeared.

Bridger, finding he had been fooled, warned his men not to venture too far from camp, and in setting their traps that night the men kept well together. A trapper by the name of Dick Owens, however, disregarded the warning, and started with his traps for a small stream about two miles distant, and did not return that night. The next morning some of the trappers went to the spot and found poor Owens killed and scalped, and Bridger discovered that the visit of the Blackfeet was only a clever trick, and that their beaver skins and village were a myth.

Our readers may perhaps think it strange that the Blackfeet, being the mortal enemies of the trappers, would so boldly venture into camp, but when it is understood that the Hudson Bay Company made them believe that any band of Indians bearing that flag could enter a white camp unmolested, it would in some measure account for their boldness. They paid a big price in beaver skins for the flag, and as the sequel proved, found that it answered the purpose. A few days after this the company moved on to the Bitter Root river, and here Rose met with an adventure that came near proving fatal to one of his companions.

Rose and Mark Head had been out on a hunt, and were returning down the river toward the camp. They had just approached a ravine when Rose, whe was riding in advance, suddenly halted. He had caught sight of a huge grizzly moving down through the bushes, on the other side of the ravine. "Mark," said Rose, pointing out the enormous animal, "there's 'Caleb,' and we might as well make four dollars this afternoon as not." (Four dollars was the price paid by the company for a grizzly's pelt.) Then slipping from his saddle he handed the bridle to Mark, and creeping through the bushes he reached a spot from where he could get a fair shot at the grizzly as he passed down the ravine. The bear soon came opposite, and not more than thirty yards distant, and Rose, raising his rifle, blazed away. At the crack of the gun the bear rolled over on his side and commenced biting furiously at the spot where the ball had entered his body.

"He's got it," said Rose, addressing his companion. "Caleb's a goner," and he at once commenced reloading his rifle.

It is an invariable custom with the western trapper or hunter after discharging his rifle to reload at once, so that he may be prepared for what may come next. The bear, after writhing and twisting for some time, contrived to scramble into a thicket of bushes, where he lay perfectly quiet.

"He's dead enough," said Rose, and we had better get to work and take off the pelt." Fastening the horses to some bushes, Mark advanced toward the thicket, and pulling the bushes to one side he called out: "All right, Rose, he's as dead as a mackerel!" and taking out his knife he seized the bear by the paw and was about to commence operations, when the bear suddenly seized him with his enormous paws, and dragging him down between his fore legs, commenced chewing his head, Mark in the meantime uttering the most fearful yells and cries for help. Rose immediately rushed forward to the spot. On reaching the bushes he saw Mark, who was now lying perfectly still, the bear still chewing away at his head. Rose immediately gave "Caleb" another shot, and succeeded this time in putting a ball through his lungs, and the bear at once commenced throwing up huge mouthfuls of blood, nearly deluging the head and shoulders of Mark. Rose now caught his companion by the legs and drew him out of the dying bear's reach.

"Are you dead, Mark?" inquired Rose, when to that gentleman's astonishment, Mark replied in rather a feeble voice:

"Purty near, I tell ye now. My head's all chawed up, an' my skull's cracked all to flinders!" Rose then led up the horses, and contrived to get Mark on one of them, but the poor fellow was too badly hurt to sit alone.

Taking both rifles, Rose got on behind Mark, so as to be able to hold him on, and leading his own horse, they started slowly for camp. Finding that Mark was likely to give out before reaching it, Rose endeavored to excite him by giving him a good scolding. He told him he had no more "grit" about him than an old squaw to let the bear handle him so roughly when he had a good knife in his hand. "Why the devil didn't you cut him all to pieces," said Rose, "and not lay there yellin' like a baby and doin' nothin'!"

"I couldn't help it," replied Mark; "when 'Caleb' gets his claws onto a feller, he's a goner, an' no mistake." Rose then asked him why he quit yelling, and laid so still.

"Well," replied Mark, "I've always hearn tell if ye lay quite still, an' the bear thinks yer dead, he won't be apt to hurt yer, so I thought I'd try it on, although every time he bit I heard my skull crackin'."

Rose contrived, however, to get his patient safely to camp. On examination the hurt appeared not so bad as was supposed. Although the skull was badly scratched and chewed, it was found not to be broken, and in a few days Mark was able to be about again.

CHAPTER XXIII.

IN WHICH ROSE AND HIS COMPANIONS START ON A BUFFALO HUNT AND ARE CHASED BY INDIANS.
A BIG FOOT RACE.

A few days after Mark Head's encounter with the bear, and when that worthy had nearly regained his accustomed health, the company broke camp and started for the Jefferson fork of the Missouri. As meat was getting a little scarce some of the trappers concluded to start on a hunt, one of the men having reported buffalo to be plentiful about ten miles up the river. Accordingly, Rose, Carson, Larrison and two Flathead Indians, took the route up the river early one morning, determined to have one or two good buffalo before night. They were also accompanied by Little Blackfoot, who, as usual, ran alongside of their horses, seeming to have no difficulty in keeping up with them.

About ten mile from camp they saw fresh buffalo sign, and leaving the river they struck out across the plain, hoping soon to come up with the game

After riding about two miles, just as they were emerging from a small hollow, they saw a herd of buffalo coming toward them at full speed. Riding into some pine bushes that grew on the side of the hill, they waited until the buffalo came within gun shot, and then blazed away, and two of the animals dropped. The herd was a small one, and at the crack of the rifles dashed furiously on and were soon out of sight.

The men proceeded at once to skin and cut up their game, when Little Blackfoot exclaimed:

"Injuns over thar!" pointing in the direction from which the trappers had come. "My people," he continued. "Me go see," and picking up his rifle he started in a lope for a hill about a mile distant.

As soon as the trappers had finished skinning and cutting up the buffalo they saw Little Blackfoot coming at full speed. On reaching the party he informed them a band of Blackfeet, numbering about forty, were hurrying down a small stream, about four miles distant, with the intention of cutting them off as they returned to camp.

The meat was immediately packed and loaded, and the trappers mounting their horses prepared to start. Little Blackfoot was told to mount one of the pack mules. This he refused to do, saying:

"Oh, me all right; they no catch Little Black-foot."

"Now, boys," said Kit Carson, "we must ride like Jehu, or we shall catch it!" and off the whole party started at full speed, which they kept up for eight miles, till they reached the spot where the small stream before mentioned emptied into the Jefferson, Rose and Kit riding ahead to reconnoiter.

Having reported "all right" the little band crossed the stream and started briskly toward the camp, the trappers wondering what had become of Little Blackfoot, whom they had not seen since they started. On arriving at the camp, they found the little runner had got there ahead of them, and they were very much astonished at the speed and bottom displayed by the little Blackfoot pedestrian.

A few days after the adventure just narrated the Hudson Bay Company paid Bridger's company a visit, and pitched their camp on a stream close by. And now commenced a scene of revelry, fun and frolic that could only be equaled at the summer rendezvous. There was plenty of horse-trading and horse-racing; shooting and wrestling matches, foot races, etc., etc. Among the Hudson Bay Company was a half-breed, who was said to be the swiftest runner in the mountains, and had already beaten anything in the Columbia valley, and this man, the Hudson Bay Company offered to back to any amount to run a foot race against any man, white or red, in Bridger's company, and they were not at all slow to accept the challenge, and Little Blackfoot was selected as their champion. Such was the confidence of Bridger's company in Little Blackfoot that they took every bet that was offered. and it soon became apparent that whichever company lost would be pretty well cleaned out, as a great many had bet nearly all they owned on the result of the race. Horses, rifles, blankets, moccasins and beads to any amount, the ground for acres being covered with the goods staked by the rival companies. Nor were the Indians less eager than their white companions to venture all they had on their favorite. The Delawares, Flatheads and Nez Perces on one side, and the Courtenies and Pondurais, who accompanied the Hudson Bay Company, on the other.

At length, everything available had been staked, the ground for the race had been selected, and the men stripped preparatory to their long run. A snowbank, plainly visible, about five miles distant, was fixed upon as the pivot around which they were to turn.

It may seem strange to some readers of this book, that a snowbank should exist in the latter part of

September, but it is a well known fact that the Rocky mountain man is scarcely ever out of sight of snow the whole year round.

The snowbank around which the men were about to run was very deep, and may have been there for ages. Running around this would make the race course about ten miles in length. About fifty men on horseback accompanied the two runners, to see that all was fair and square, and Little Blackfoot and the half-breed started in fine style for their ten mile run.

The Blackfoot had provided himself with a small willow switch, with which he playfully tapped the legs of his companion as he ran along by his side.

The two men kept well together till they reached the snowbank, and such was their astonishing speed, that the horsemen were compelled to go in a constant lope to keep up with them. After turning the snowbank, Little Blackfoot began to forge ahead. When within two miles of camp he was at least half a mile ahead of the half-breed who, having exerted himself too much, fell to the ground and was obliged to be brought to the camp on horse back.

"See here, boys," said Kit Carson, who was a good runner, "I'm goin' to beat Little Blackfoot for once. Let's go out and meet him."

Accordingly, Carson, Rose and two or three other trappers went about three hundred yards and waited till the Blackfoot came up, when they all started with him for the camp. But even after running the ten miles Little Blackfoot was too much for any of them, beating them into camp with the greatest ease.

There was much rejoicing among Bridger's company at the result of the race, and a great deal of valuable property changed hands.

The half-breed said that when the Blackfoot touched him on the legs with the switch he bewitched or charmed him, thereby causing him to lose the race, and the Hudson Bay Company seemed inclined to test the fairness of the race on this ground, but finding Bridger's company too strong and determined for them, were compelled at length to acknowledge themselves beaten.

Rose says this was the most exciting scene he ever witnessed during his stay in the Rockies, and from that time forward Little Blackfoot was considered a hero among them.

The Hudson Bay Company soon after left, and Bridger trapped up Jefferson Fork till the latter end of October, when they started across the mountains for the headquarters of Snake river, where they intended to trap until they went into winter quarters.

It is well known that the climate is warmer on the west slope of the mountains than on the east slope, and that consequently the trappers are enabled to carry on their business much later in the fall on the streams of the western slope. Added to this, Fort Hall was still in existence, and this would be an advantage to the trappers, as, if at any time they were in need of fresh stores they could be procured at the Fort.

CHAPTER XXIV.

IN WHICH ROSE HAD A SINGULAR ADVENTURE WITH A GRIZZLY—SCARCITY OF PROVISIONS IN CAMP. HUNTING PARTY NEARLY STARVED. BLACKFOOT SPY.

The spot selected for winter quarters was about four miles from Fort Hall, and although very advantageous in some respects it was very deficient in others. There was plenty of timber and cottonwood for the horses, but owing to the near proximity of Fort Hall, game was very scarce, the men belonging to the Fort having scared it away from the neighborhood. Hunters would often start out and be gone for days together and would return empty handed.

One morning Rose, mounted on a mule, was slowly wending his way up one of the streams a few miles from camp, in the hopes of falling in with a deer or buffalo. As he was crossing a little knoll he saw, about two hundred yards ahead of him, a large grizzly, and not wishing to lose the opportunity of making four dollars, the sum paid for the skins, he determined to try a shot at "Caleb." Hitching his mule in a grove of pine bushes, he moved slowly and cautiously toward the bear until he reached a small clump of willows about fifty yards from the animal, who was standing with his head turned away and in the right position for a good shot. Rose's first care was to look around for some tree into which he could climb if his shot did not prove successful. About ten yards from him were two tall, slim cottonwoods growing close together, and up either of which he would be able to climb out of the bear's reach if necessary. Feeling now that he had a safe retreat within reach, he raised his rifle and took deliberate aim, but just as he pulled the trigger the bear suddenly turned towards him, and the ball, instead of entering a vital part, struck him in the shoulder. Seeing that his shot was unsuccessful Rose made for the cottonwoods, and immediately climbed one of them, and "Caleb" catching sight of him, rushed savagely toward him. Rose had dropped his rifle, and this the bear instantly seized, and in two minutes had the stock chewed all to pieces. He then made for the cottonwoods, and raising himself on his hind legs tried to reach Rose. Finding this could not be done, he wedged himself between the two saplings, which were about two feet apart, and placing his back against one, he pushed his immense paws against the other with all his might. The saplings being slim bent fearfully, and Rose fancied he heard the one on which he was perched beginning to crack, and had about concluded it was all over for him, when by good fortune the back of the bear slipped off the sapling against which he was pressing, and he fell to the ground. This so demoralized him that he at once gave up the contest, making his way slowly up the stream, and was soon lost in the bushes.

Rose descended from his sapling, and picking up his now useless rifle, he mounted his mule and started for camp, rejoicing at his fortunate escape. This little affair cost him a new rifle.

About the middle of January affairs began to assume rather a gloomy aspect. Provisions were getting rather scarce, and the weather was so bad the men could not get out to hunt. At length, finding it would be impossible to go any longer without a supply of food, Rose, Meek, Larrison, Burrows, and a Flathead Indian started off one morning in an easterly direction, determined to have game of some kind, if within the bounds of possibility. The day was stormy and the snow was falling fast, and their progress was consequently slow, the snow being often belly deep to their horses. Toward night they reached some small, deserted Indian huts, and here they resolved to camp.

Having gathered a quantity of cottonwood bark for their horses, they built a roaring fire in one of the huts, and rolling themselves in their buffalo skins they laid down to sleep, not having tasted food that day.

The next morning the weather was worse, if possible, than the day before. The wind was blowing a perfect gale, and the snow came down so thick and fast that it was impossible to see one rod ahead. Several times Rose and his companions tried to get out and hunt up something to eat, but found it utterly impossible. They still, however, contrived to get bark enough for their horses, and the second night was passed without eating a bite.

The men were now actually in a starving condition, and they came to the determination that if

nothing turned up the next day they would be
compelled to kill one of their horses.

The next morning was fine, although the wind
was still blowing, and after feeding their animals
the men started once more to try their luck. About
a mile from the huts Burrows caught sight of a
raven in a cottonwood tree, and he informed his
companions he was going to kill it, as a raven was
better than nothing. Just then the men saw what
appeared to be a heavy rolling cloud of snow coming toward them with the wind, and they knew at
once what it was. It was a herd of buffalo rushing
along, plowing and tossing the snow in every
direction in their headlong flight. The buffalo
and snow were so mixed up that it was impossible
to take aim and the men fired into the herd hap-
hazzard. Fortunately one of the shots broke the
back of a large cow, and the hunters proceeded at
once to skin the animal. Such was their intense
hunger that some of them commenced eating the
buffalo raw, and instead of taking the choicest
parts, as they had been in the habit of doing, they
cut up and packed the whole carcass, and the day
was spent in roasting and eating buffalo, the men
seeming as if they could not possibly eat enough
after their long fast. The next day they started
for camp, delighting their comrades with a supply

of fresh meat of which they were so much in need.

In February the weather proved to be much finer, and the trappers being now better able to travel contrived to keep the camp well supplied with provisions. Some of the trappers would occasionally visit Fort Hall. The men at the Fort had experienced the same difficulty as Bridger's company, but they congratulated themselves on one thing, they had not been molested by the Blackfeet during the winter. Soon after the ice went off, about the beginning of April, Rose and two of the trappers had gone down to Fort Hall. While there a half-breed made his appearance on the opposite side of the river, and called to the men to bring the canoe across as he had some beaver skins he wished to trade. Rose told the men to be careful, informing them, if he was not mistaken, the half-breed was a rascal by the name of Bird, who was known to be connected with the Blackfeet.

After some little parley, two of the men belonging to Fort Hall volunteered to take the canoe across, but scarcely had they landed on the other side when they were surrounded by Blackfeet Indians, killed and scalped, the Indians shaking the scalps triumphantly at the white men on the other side of the river. Several shots were fired at them, but the distance was too great to do any serious damage.

April set in warm and pleasant, and Bridger and his company were making preparations to commence the spring trapping. Just before breaking camp they were joined by several Nez Perces Indians, who informed them that the small-pox had been very bad among the Blackfeet, and that a great many of that nation had died. They also informed the company that several bands of Crows had been seen on the Gallatin river.

The Crows are not considered as deadly enemies as the Blackfeet. They appear to be a little more civilized, and take white men prisoners. The Blackfeet, on the contrary, never take any prisoners, but kill and scalp all who are so unfortunate as to fall into their hands.

Fearing that they would be likely to have trouble with the Indians, Bridger resolved to cross the mountains and push right through the Blackfoot country, having heard there were plenty of beaver between the Gallatin and Madison rivers.

CHAPTER XXV.

IN WHICH ROSE LEAVES THE COMPANY ON A TRAP-
PING EXPEDITION—TAKEN PRISONER BY THE CROWS.

Finding the season sufficiently advanced Bridger and his company started on the spring hunt for beaver, intending to cross the mountains by the way of Lake Henry.

There are three passes in the mountains gener-ally used by the trappers. The most northern pass is known as the Red Rocks Pass. The pass by the way of Lake Henry is the middle pass. South of this is Teton's, which we have before described. After remaining a few days at Lake Henry the company proceeded to Jackson's Lake, about forty miles distant. Rose, finding they were likely to be a little too much crowded, and knowing he always succeeded in taking more skins when sepa-rated from the company, resolved to leave and carry on the spring hunt alone, with the intention of not joining the company till they met at the rendezvous.

Among his companions were two trappers named Allen and Gordon. These men, either through fear or caution, would never trap at any great dis-tance from camp, and consequently had never met with any of the adventures or hair-breadth escapes common to trappers who go it alone. This spring, however, having listened to the glowing accounts of the large number of beaver taken by small parties of trappers, and also having great confidence in Rose, who, since winning the prize, was considered quite an expert, they prayed very hard to be allowed to accompany him. To this Rose at length consented, and one morning the three mounted their horses and started for the Wind River Mountains, intending to make the first attempt on the tributaries of the Wind and Powder rivers. We may here mention there is another river in that locality called by the trappers "Stinking" river, or Bad Water. On this stream no beaver were ever seen or caught. The water is strongly impregnated with carbon oil, and quantities of it may always be seen floating on its surface.

The third day after reaching Jackson's Lake, Rose and his companions reached a spur of the Wind River Mountain, which they found it necessary to ascend. The buffalo trail which they followed was so narrow they had to walk Indian file, and in some places the path was so steep they were compelled to dismount and lead their horses. When near the top a flock of mountain sheep came rushing toward them. Rose succeeded in shooting one of these animals, and on reaching the top of the mountain a fire was kindled, and the three made an excellent repast on the mountain mutton. Having concluded their meal they once more mounted their horses. Before them was a large stretch of sage prairie, and after riding a mile or so Rose perceived in the distance what he supposed to be a herd of elk. His reason for supposing it to be these animals was that he could see spots of white, and as the hinder parts of elk are white, they naturally concluded they were about to come across a herd of these splendid specimens of the deer tribe. They appeared to be coming rapidly towards them; but owing to the height of the sage bushes, it was almost impossible to see distinctly where they were. At length Rose, who had been keeping his eye on them, suddenly halted.

"Boys," said he, "they are men on horseback, and Indians at that, and I think it most likely Blackfeet. We shall have to ride for it now," and wheeling their horses they started back, and down the mountain at a breakneck pace, the Indians coming on in swift pursuit, and on reaching the bottom of the mountain, the Indians had gained on them to such an extent, they found it would be impossible to escape. Leaving their horses at the foot of a rocky hill, they ascended to the top, and commenced building a breast work of loose rocks, resolving to sell their lives as dearly as possible. As this was Allen's and Gordon's first adventure, they were pretty badly scared, and handled the rocks lively for some time.

As soon as the Indians reached the foot of the hill, on the top of which Rose and his companions were entrenching themselves, one of the number, who appeared to be the chief, stripped himself and ascended the hill towards them.

"Rose," said Gordon, rising his rifle, "if that fellow comes ten steps nearer, I'll shoot him!"

"See here," said Rose, "If you shoot that Indian, I'll shoot you. If you kill him, we're all dead men. Now just let me run this thing," continued Rose, "and if there's any possibility of getting out of this scrape, I'll do it."

The Indian had now advanced to within fifty yards of the entrenchment, and Rose, divesting himself of his apparel, advanced to meet him in the old Adamite costume, minus the fig leaves.

It is the custom among the Indians, when men of two contending parties meet for the purpose of holding a "pow-wow," they come forth naked, so as to show that they do not carry any concealed weapons.

Rose stepped boldly up to the Indian, and after the usual salutation, "Hello!" he at once made the inquiry:

"Who are you?"

The Indian informed him he belonged to the Crow nation. At this Rose expressed the most unbounded delight. He told the warrior he and his companions were in search of his people; that the "white chief" had sent them, and that the company would be along in three days with a large quantity of blankets, powder, lead, beads, guns, etc., etc., which they wished to trade for beaver skins; and that when they at first saw them on the mountain, they had taken them to be Blackfeet, who were their mortal enemies, and that was the reason they had tried to get away from them. He then showed him his wounded arm, telling him he had received the wound from the Blackfeet, that he had killed many of their nation, and hoped to kill many more, and that the Black- feet were dogs, All this he said because he knew the Blackfeet to be the mortal enemies of the Crows. Rose was an excellent sign talker, and as the Crow chief knew a few words of English, and Rose could speak a little Indian, he contrived to make the chief understand all he wished him to know.

The Crow appeared to be much pleased to hear that the white chief was coming on with goods, and still more delighted to find the white men were such bitter enemies to the Blackfeet. He told Rose to bring on his companions and his band would hold a "pow-wow" on what should be done with them. Rose accordingly went back to his friends, told them what had passed between him and the chief.

"Now, boys," said Rose, as he resumed his apparel, "you must go with me to the Crow camp, and try and put a good face on the matter and it will be all the better for us."

"Yes," replied Gordon, "I know just how it will be. When they get us down there they'll murder every mother's son of us."

"Well," said Rose, "we can't get away from them, so I think we had better put a bold face on the matter, and all may come right." The three men then started down the hill to the Crow camp, and were at once surrounded by the Indians, who formed a ring, placing them in the center.

The chief who had met Rose now commenced a long harangue, in which he informed them of all that Rose had told him.

Gordon and Allen, who were scared nearly out of their senses, looked on this ceremony with pale faces.

"Rose," said Gordon, "as soon as that fellow gets through they'll murder us."

Rose endeavored to keep their spirits up by telling them it was all right.

As soon as the chief was done speaking two or three of the other warriors spoke, seeming to assent to some proposition the chief had made.

The band consisted of about sixty young men and boys, and they seemed to be much pleased with the idea of trading with the white men, and the chief informed Rose they had concluded to take them to the village.

Rose told them it would be necessary to let the white chief know that they were willing to trade. and for this purpose they had better let his two companions return to the camp. This the Crow chief agreed to, and their horses having been brought up, Allen and Gordon left the Crow camp.

At first they rode slowly, but still having an idea the Indians intended to play them some trick, they went faster and faster, and the last Rose saw of them they were going at their utmost speed.

The Indians, accompanied by Rose, now started for the Crow village, which the chief had before informed him was about three days' journey from that place.

After again ascending the mountain they rode several miles across the prairie, when the chief called a halt, ordering his men to remain where they were. Then, accompanied by Rose, he rode some distance from the others, and pausing, he pointed to his tongue and spread out two of his fingers, meaning he had been speaking with a forked tongue, or lying to him; that instead of the Crow village being three days' journey distant, they were now close upon it, and riding on a few hundred yards to the edge of the hill, he saw before him the Crow village not more than half a mile distant.

CHAPTER XXVI.

IN WHICH ROSE ENTERS THE CROW VILLAGE—WIT-
NESSES THE GREAT INDIAN GAME OF "HANDS,"
IS ADOPTED INTO THE TRIBE.

The Indian village on which they gazed seemed but just commenced, as only five or six lodges were up, although several more were in the process of erection.

In forming an Indian village the lodges are placed in a circle so as to enclose about two acres of ground, into which the horses are driven at night for safe keeping. Rose asked the chief how many lodges the village would contain when completed. To this he replied by holding up both hands and spreading out his fingers twenty times, thereby indicating the village would consist of about two hundred lodges. Rose and the chief now started toward the village, and on entering it the Indian commenced a loud harangue. This brought together all the dogs, squaws and warriors, who followed them to the chief's lodge. The old chief hearing the noise soon made his appearance. He was quite a remarkable personage—tall, athletic, and about seventy years of age. But his most remarkable peculiarity was the immense length of his hair, which had given him the name of "Long Hair." Bridger, who had often seen him, declared it was fourteen feet long. This story, however was scarcely believed, and Rose had now an opportunity of seeing it himself. It hung down his back nearly to his heels in a thick roll, stuck together at intervals of about a foot and a half with pitch, and tied with a buckstring whang. From his heels his hair was again turned up to the back of his neck and again fell nearly to his heels, making three lengths of between four and five feet each, showing that when stretched out to its full length it would be fully as long as Bridger pronounced it. As soon as the old chief made his appearance the young one commenced an harangue, and although Rose did not understand the language, he knew he was giving a full description of the capture of himself and companions, together with all that had passed between them.

As soon as the young chief had finished, the old one commenced, and Rose soon ascertained that it was for the purpose of calling the warrors together in council to determine what should be done with the prisoner. When the chief concluded, Rose was taken into the lodge, and was soon followed by all the principal warriors, who seated themselves in a circle on the ground. The medicine pipe was then lit, and was slowly passed from one to the other, each taking a draw. As soon as this ceremony was completed the old chief arose and made a long speech, in which he informed them of all that had occurred, and his own views on the subject. Several of the other warriors arose and made shorter speeches, when the council was adjourned, and Rose was informed that no other action would be taken until the three days had expired, at which time the arrival of Bridger was expected.

Rose passed that night in the lodge of the chief, but he scarcely slept a wink. In the next lodge to the one he occupied there was a fearful racket going on. Singing, shouting and beating of sticks, and Rose thought it was all done on account of his being taken prisoner. But the next morning the young chief informed him that the great Indian game of "hands" had been going on in the adjoining lodge.

As soon as they had eaten breakfast that morning, the old chief and Rose, mounted on two splendid horses, commenced riding around the village. They paused at every lodge, and the old chief made a short introductory speech. Some ceremonies were gone through, and cakes were brought out by the squaws, which, Rose understood, he was expected to eat. These cakes were made of pounded berries, roots and dried buffalo meat, made up and dried in the sun. After going the morning rounds, Rose was allowed to amuse himself around the village the balance of the day, but never alone.

Almost every hour fresh lodges were arriving, and Rose discovered the young chief was right as to the size of the village. At night, he saw they were again gathering in the lodge for another game of "hands," and much to his satisfaction, he was invited by the young chief to witness it. The lodge was soon filled with as many warriors and squaws as could be conveniently seated. These were divided into two parties, warriors and squaws being on each side, and three or four experts were selected from each party to carry on the game.

Some of these were squaws, who, the young chief informed him, were often more expert at the game than men. A pole was laid on the ground between the contending parties. One of the persons selected now commenced the game, taking in his hand a small piece of polished bone, of an oval shape, and resembling the handle of a small gimlet. This bone he placed between his two hands, and now the game commenced, by moving his hands rapidly to and fro, up and down, but always in front of him, so that they could be seen by the opposing party. Suddenly his hands would close and separate, and he would then hold them up. If any one on the other side felt pretty sure they could tell which hand the bone was in, they would point to it. If successful, they would receive a stick. If they missed they would have to give one, twenty-one sticks being the game. Sometimes the manipulator of the bone would hold up his hands half a dozen times before any one would venture to guess. In the meantime betting of every description was going on both by squaws and warriors. The stakes were generally beads, moccasins, leggins, blankets, etc., etc. As soon as the bet was made, the stakes were laid together near the dividing pole, under the care of some responsible person. When the game commenced, the parties all began to sing, keeping time by beating on the ridge pole that ran across the tent. The songs consisted of words improvised by some of the warriors, and a sort of a chorus joined in by the whole company.

This game sometimes took the whole night to play, one party sometimes gaining nineteen or twenty sticks, when the luck would change, and the other side possibly become the winners. The great art in this game is to make the beholders believe that they can actually see the bone in one hand, when it is really in the other.

The second day Rose accompanied some of the braves on a hunt, and as the Crows were not very expert with the rifle, Rose determined to show them a little good shooting. In the afternoon an antelope was seen standing about a hundred and fifty yards distant. Holding up his hand as a sign for the Indians to stop, Rose dismounted from his horse, stuck his ramrod into the ground, and resting his rifle on it took deliberate aim at the top of the animal's head, so as to allow for the great distance. At the crack of the rifle the antelope dropped, shot through the breast, much to the astonishment of the warriors who accompanied Rose, and this lucky shot raised him very much in the estimation of the tribe, who were soon told of the circumstance, and he was considered by them as a dead shot and a great hunter.

The three days had now passed, and, as Rose was fully aware, Bridger did not make his appearance. A party had been sent out to meet him and bring him to the village, but they returned stating that the white chief was no where in the neighborhood. Rose pretended to be very angry, and said that as the white chief had lied to him he would have nothing more to do with him, and would henceforward make his home with the Crow nation. He pointed out to the old chief the advantage it would be to him and his people to take him as a member of their tribe. He showed them how they were cheated in trading with the whites; that instead of getting ten bullets and ten charges of powder for a beaver skin, they ought to get at least a hundred times as much; and that instead of giving ten beaver skins for a fusee, they were only worth one, and everything else in proportion; and that if they concluded to take him as a member of their tribe he would henceforward do their trading and see that they got the worth of their pelts.

After some "pow-wowing" the old chief and his warriors not only agreed to adopt him into the tribe, but also informed him that he would give him his only daughter for a wife. The young girl was called "White Cloud," principally on account of her skin being fairer than the generality of the squaws, and he told Rose, who was called "Sueappie," or white, that his daughter was also "Sueappie," meaning that she, too, was white.

As soon as it was known that Rose was to become a member of their tribe, the squaws went to work to pull out his beard by the roots, using his bullet moulds as tweezers; and Rose says, though he did not have much beard, his face was kept sore for some time.

Rose now hit on a great stroke of diplomacy. He told the Indians he had several beautiful red horses (bay being the color most esteemed among the Crows). One of these he intended to present to his father-in-law, the old chief, and one to each of his intended brothers-in-law. He also told them he intended to make them each a present of a rifle. But to do this it would be necessary for him to go to the white camp and bring away all the property belonging to him there.

After some considerable "pow-wowing" it was agreed that Rose should return to his white friends, get all his property, and on his return the marriage between himself and "White Cloud" should be celebrated at once, and he should from that time be a "Sueappie" chief in the Crow nation.

CHAPTER XXVII.

IN WHICH THE CROW CAMP, ACCOMPANIED RY ROSE,
MOVES ON TO THE BIG HORN—ROSE LEAVES THE
TRIBE, FINDS BRIDGER'S TRAIL, AND
JOINS HIS COMPANY.

The chiefs and warriors belonging to the Crow tribe held several "pow-wows" for the purpose of discussing Rose's intended visit to his company, they having not yet appointed the time for him to leave. "Long Hair," the chief, however, was a man whose word could be thoroughly depended on, and his word was law among his people. Rose says he was the most conscientious man he ever met with, and nothing would tempt him to commit an act that he thought would anger the Great Spirit. He told Rose that in his youth he had gone into the mountains seven days and prayed to the Great Spirit to give him the longest hair of any living man, and that the Great Spirit had granted his request.

As the pasture was getting scarce around the Crow village it was determined to strike the lodges and move on to the Big Horn, and accordingly the tenth day after he was taken prisoner, Rose, in company with the tribe, started for that stream. Rose had become a great favorite with the young warriors, he having taught them to shoot with the rifle. The arms of the Crows consisted of bows and arrows, spears, and a few fusees, and until Rose's capture they had never had a rifle among them, and they were much astonished with the accuracy displayed by Rose in shooting with that weapon, and were pleased to be allowed to try their skill, and in return, they taught Rose to shoot with the bow and arrow.

"White Cloud," Rose's intended bride, together with other Indian maidens, would sometimes come out to see the sport. Now, although Rose pretended to be delighted with the prospect of becoming a "Sueappie" chief, and a son-in-law to the renowned "Long Hair," yet he could not conscientiously say to the maiden, as Ruth said to Naomi: "Thy people shall be my people, and thy God my God," and although he acknowledges he had a good time among the Crows, still the thoughts of home, relations, friends, and the comrades with whom he had so recently parted, would rise up before him, and he longed once more to be among his own people.

On the fourteenth day of his captivity they pitched their tents on the banks of the Big Horn, and Rose accompanied the young braves on several hunting expeditions, during which he had numer-

ous opportunities of escaping; but, as bands of
Blackfeet were known to be in the neighborhood,
and, as an unsuccessful attempt would place him
in a worse position than he was at present, he
determined to bide his time, and wait for the old
chief's permission to depart. At length, one morning, the old chief called him into his tent, and after
questioning him closely as to the amount of property he possessed in his own company, and whether
it would be worth the risk of a solitary and dangerous tramp through the Blackfeet country, the
old chief advised him to give it up, and settle
down with them at once as one of their tribe; but
Rose informed the chief he could not do this without letting his company know, as he had signed
articles with them, and the Great Spirit would be
angry if he did not inform them of his intention.
He furthermore stated he had a good horse and
was not afraid of the Blackfeet, and that the
property he possessed in his own company was too
valuable to be given up for the sake of a little risk
and a few days ride.

The chief then informed him that he should
start the next morning, and that his son "Rain,"
that being the name of the young chief who had
captured him, together with a number of the
young braves, should accompany him on his first
day's journey.

Early the next morning Rose's horse was brought to him, this being the first time he had ridden the animal since his capture. At the back of his saddle, instead of his traps, was a large bag containing presents for the white chief, and which Rose afterward discovered was filled with beautifully worked moccasins, leggins, and belts, and after a great leave-taking with the tribe, Rose started in the direction of Clark's Fork, accompanied by the young chief "Rain," and about twenty of the braves. At night they camped on Clark's Fork, and before going to sleep the young chief gave Rose a good deal of advice as to his future mode of proceeding. He informed him that bands of Blackfeet were numerous in that part of the country, and that it would be better for him to lay up in the day time and travel at night, and that if he should be compelled to make a fire to cook something to eat, he must on no account camp near it, but be sure and put several miles between it and his camping ground.

The next morning Rose shook hands with the braves, and lastly with the chief, to whom he had become much attached. As the young Indian grasped him by the hand, and looking earnestly in his face, said: " 'Seappie,' I shall never see you again;" but Rose merely laughed, and told him he would see him again before one moon, and so they parted. The young chief's words being prophetic, they never met again.

Rose, being now left to himself, took his solitary way across the plains with the intention of making his way toward Jackson Lake, where he expected to fall in with his company. He moved along very cautiously, taking advantage of every hill or rise in the ground to reconnoitre, knowing he was in continual danger of falling in with the Blackfeet. On the afternoon of that day he struck the company's trail, and after following it for some little time he discovered that another and fresher trail had joined it. The latter he knew at once to be Indians, and as the marks of their moccasined feet appeared to be quite fresh, he knew the Indians were not far off, and he at once concealed himself in a grove of bushes where he lay by till night. As soon as darkness had set in he again started on his journey, and knowing well the direction the company would take, he followed on in that direction until day began to break, when he again took to cover. After picketing his horse where it could get plenty of good grass, he lay down and slept till noon, then going to the top of a small hill close by, he examined the route he was about to take closely, and seeing nothing suspicious, determined to proceed on his journey. Just before night he found that the trail led across a small stream, bordered with willows and pines, and he thought this would be an excellent place for an Indian ambush. But Rose was not to be caught napping. He rode along apparently unconscious until he came within about one hundred and fifty yards of the bushes, when he suddenly wheeled his horse and started at full gallop up the stream, until he discovered a good crossing place. On reaching the opposite bank he again started at full speed to once more regain the trail, which he soon did and followed it till nightfall. Hearing or seeing nothing of the Indians, he kindled a small fire among the bushes and roasted some buffalo steak, cooking enough to last him a couple of days, and mounting his horse he rode about three miles farther on and camped for the night. The next morning he again took up the trail, and just before the middle of the day he discovered where Bridger's company had camped the night previous, some of the fires being not yet extinguished. It was a very stony, gravelly place where the company had camped, and Rose found it almost impossible to discover the trail. He at first took a circuit of about a mile around the camp, then increased the distance to two, and then to three or four miles, and at length, to his great delight, succeeded in striking it just before nightfall. He rode on rapidly for two hours; then thinking that if the Blackfeet were still on the tráil, he must be pretty close upon them, he determined to camp for the night. The next morning, seeing a hill about four or five miles distant, he rode toward it. Near the foot of the hill was a growth of scrubby pines. Here he hitched his horse and ascended to reconnoiter. After staying there for some considerable time, he saw two men on horseback coming toward him, but could not tell whether they were white men or Indians, and Rose felt very anxious as he lay there watching their approach. Some times as they rode one behind the other, he would feel almost sure they were Blackfeet. Then, again, as they rode side by side, his hopes would revive, and he felt almost positive they were his own people. At length they came so close that he could see the wolf-skin cap and long beard of the trappers, and springing to his feet he shot off his gun, waved his cap, and the two men came galloping toward him. They proved to be two of Bridger's company, John Hawkins and Charley Wafield, who were delighted at once more meeting their old comrade. They informed Rose that Allen and Gordon had returned and given the boys a full account of their capture by the Crows, and that he (Rose) had been given up as lost.

The three men then returned to camp, which was not more than five miles distant. Great was the astonishment and rejoicing in camp when Rose made his appearance, and many were the questions asked on every side, and Rose was compelled to relate his adventures over and over again to a delighted and sympathetic audience. Bridger, too, was pleased to have the story of the chief's long hair corroborated, as many of the trappers had considered it a myth.

The excitement, however, gradually wore down, and Rose once more took his accustomed place among the trappers.

CHAPTER XXVIII.

THE RENDEZVOUS, ARRIVAL OF GRAND VISITORS, TRIP TO WIND RIVER, FIGHT WITH THE BLACKFEET.

The season being now far advanced, and time for the rendezvous nearly at hand, Bridger and his company left Jackson's Hole and commenced moving toward Green River, trapping as they went. It was during this trip that Rose met with a rather curious adventure, and had, what might be called a very narrow escape. The ground over which they had been traveling for some days, was so stony, or gravelly, it was very hard on the horses feet; in fact, some of them became so sore they could hardly travel, and the trappers were compelled to make moccasins for them out of raw hide, and Rose, wishing to make up for lost time, determined to try his luck on a small stream, on which beaver were said to be plenty; but the spot was known to be infested by Blackfeet, and few of the trappers felt inclined to venture in that direction.

As the horse belonging to Rose was too lame to travel, he started on an old mule belonging to the company, and Rose says it was one of the most stubborn brutes he ever saw. No amount of coaxing, whipping, or spurring would induce it to get out of a walk; in fact, when he felt the spur touch his flanks, he would stop at once and commence biting at the rider's feet; but, as the mule's hoofs were sound, Rose concluded that anything would be better than walking. He felt convinced, however, that if chased by the Blackfeet, he should be compelled to leave the mule and trust to his own legs for safety.

About five miles from camp he shot a deer, and taking from it the fat ribs, he cooked enough to do him a day or two, taking the balance along in case he should need it. A little after nightfall he reached his destination, and as beaver signs were good, he at once set his traps, hung his venison on a bush, tethered his mule, and rolling himself in his blankets laid down in the bushes and went to sleep. How long he slept he didn't know. He was suddenly awakened by the snorting of the mule, and springing to his feet, rifle in hand, he saw a large grizzly bear walking off with his venison. Cocking his rifle, he was about to fire, when "Caleb" disappeared in the bushes. It being too dark to follow the monster, Rose again laid down, and slept till near daylight, then taking up his traps he discovered he had caught four good beaver. While engaged in skinning them he fancied he smelt the smoke of a fire, and hurrying up the skinning process, he packed his traps, and mounting his mule, rode out of the bushes to a small hill close by. From the top of this, he was horrified to perceive a camp of nearly two hundred Blackfeet Indians, not more than two hundred yards above him on the stream. It being still dark, Rose had not been seen, and he immediately started for the camp, expecting to hear the howling savages on his trail.

On reaching a hill near his own camp, he saw two Indians lying flat on the ground, reconnoitering. Rose felt certain he could kill one of them, but then what was to prevent the other one from killing him? Just as he was considering what was best to be done, the Indians caught sight of him, and springing to their feet, ran off at full speed, and Rose rode into camp with his old mule and his beaver skins, thinking he had had a very narrow escape.

The rendezvous of '37 was a very grand affair, and the new supply of stores was very much needed. The company had done a great deal of trading during the year, and their stock of goods had been nearly exhausted for some time; in fact, the trappers had never been in as bad a fix since their trip to the Humboldt river. Their blankets were worn out, and their ammunition was getting low, and Bridger began to get scared, as an encounter with the Blackfeet, under the circumstances, would have been dangerous. But the caravan from St. Louis made its appearance at about the usual time, and laughter, fun and frolic were once more the order of the day.

Several visitors came out with the train from St. Louis this year. Mr. Grey, the missionary, returned to the mountains, bringing with him his wife and four other ladies, all bound for the mission on the Columbia river. An English nobleman, known as Sir William Stewart, called by the trappers Captain Stewart, also came out with the train, bringing with him a retinue of servants, and a number of splendid horses. This was Captain Stewart's second trip to the mountains, he having been delighted with his first visit. He brought with him lots of stores, and regaled the whole of the trappers with a grand entertainment. He also made them some very valuable presents, giving Bridger, Carson and Meek, with whom he had become acquainted on his first visit, each a valuable horse, and to many of the other trappers he gave costly presents. It was at this entertainment that Rose partook of some water and crackers, this being the first thing of the kind he had eaten since his stay in the mountains, and the boys all thought it a great delicacy.

The Delaware and Shawnee Indians came in large number to trade; and that summer Bridger sent over a hundred packs of beaver skins to St. Louis, together with a large quantity of buffalo robes and grizzly pelts. There was the usual amount of drinking, carousing, horse-racing, etc., and altogether the rendezvous of this year presented a remarkably lively appearance. When the rendezvous was pretty well over, and the time for fall trapping was drawing near, Bridger and Dripps

called in Rose and Carson for the purpose of holding a "pow-wow" as to the route it would be best
to take for the fall hunt. Rose was in favor of the
Wind river, as beaver were known to be plentiful
in all the streams that took their rise in the Wind
river mountains. But to reach this desirable
location it would be necessary to pass through the
heart of the Blackfoot country, and in all probability they would have to do some tall fighting.
But as the idea of a fight with the Blackfeet was
not likely to prove an objection to their taking
that route—that, in fact, to many of the trappers it
would be an inducement—it was agreed by Bridger
and his partner that the Wind river should be the
scene of operations for the first part of the fall
hunt.

All things being now in readiness, Bridger and
his company started for the Wind river mountains,
and nothing of interest occurred for the first two or
three days. On the fourth day, however, Rose,
Meek, and about thirty or forty of the other trappers, set out to travel up the river to headwaters,
accompanied by the famous Indian painter, Stanley,
whose party was met with, this fall, traveling
among the mountains. The party of trappers were
a day or two ahead of the main camp, when they
found themselves following close after the big

Blackfoot village, which had recently passed over the trail, as could be seen by the usual signs, also, by the dead bodies strewn along the trail, victims to that horrible scourge, smallpox. The village was evidently fleeing to the mountains, hoping to rid itself of the plague in their colder and more salubrious air. Not long after coming on these evidences of proximity to an enemy, a party of a hundred and fifty of their warriors were discovered encamped in a defile, or narrow bottom, enclosed by high bluffs, through which the trappers would have to pass. Seeing that in order to pass the war party, and the village, which was about half a mile in advance, there would have to be some fighting done, the trappers resolved to begin the battle at once by attacking their enemies, who were as yet ignorant of their presence in the neighborhood. In pursuance of this determination, Rose, Meek Newell, Mansfield and Le Blas commenced hostilities. Leaving their horses in camp, they crawled along on the edge of the overhanging bluff until opposite to the encampment of Blackfeet, firing on them from the shelter of some bushes which grew among the rocks. But the Blackfeet, though ignorant of the number of their enemies, were not to be dislodged so easily, and after an hour or two of random shooting contrived to scale the bluffs at a point higher up, and to get upon a ridge of ground still higher than that occupied by the trappers. This movement dislodged the latter, and they hastily retreated through the bushes and returned to camp.

The next day, the main camp having come up, the fight was renewed. While the greater body of the company, with the pack horses, were passing along the high bluffs overhanging them, the party of the day before and forty or fifty others, undertook to drive the Indians from the bottom, and by keeping them engaged, allow the train to pass in safety. This they contrived to do, and after some heavy skirmishing the Indians were compelled to retreat to their village, and Bridger and his company continued to Wind river without meeting with any further adventure.

CHAPTER XXIX.

THE FALL HUNT—AMMUNITION RUNS SHORT—ROSE
VOLUNTEERS TO GO TO FORT LARAMIE—HIS
ADVENTURES WITH THE GROVOUTS,
AND SAFE RETURN.

The fall hunt did not prove as successful as was anticipated. Although beaver were plentiful on the Wind river, the company were continually annoyed by prowling bands of Blackfeet, who were hovering around the camp, in the hopes of cutting off some straggling trapper, or stampeding and stealing some of the horses. This annoyance interfered considerably with the trapping business, as they were compelled to hunt in strong squads. Even then they would often lose some of their traps. This was not at all a healthy situation for the trappers to be placed in; but it was still more unhealthy for the Blackfeet, several of whom were caught sneaking around the camp and sent to the happy hunting grounds by the deadly rifle of the trapper. To add to their misfortune and annoyance it was found that their ammunition was running short, and it would be impossible for them to continue on unless a fresh supply could be obtained from some quarter. In fact, Bridger began to get very uneasy, and towards the latter end of October, he sent Tom Biggs with ten men and some pack horses, to Fort Laramie, to procure the needed supplies, and with strict orders to return with them at once before winter set in; but, unfortunately, cold and story weather came on early that winter, and about the middle of November the company proceeded to their winter quarters on the Yellowstone.

The latter end of November, the winter appeared

to set in in thorough earnest. . There were continual and heavy snow storms, and all the streams in that region were frozen over.

Biggs and his party had been given up for some time, as it would be impossible for horses to travel through the snow, and Bridger began to be very much alarmed for the safety of the company.

Several consultations were held as to what was best to be done under the circumstances. Bridger thought that Biggs and his company had been gobbled up by the Indians, or he would most assuredly have been back before winter set in. At length Rose volunteered to go to Fort Laramie, if one of the other trappers would accompany him; but this, at first, none of them seem inclined to do. But after two days consideration, a trapper by the name of David Woods volunteered to go, and it was agreed that Rose and Woods should start the next morning.

The accoutrements for their journey consisted, besides their rifles and ammunition, of a buffalo robe and a blanket for each, and a pair of snow shoes. Thus equipped, and provided with two days' rations of buffalo meat, they started on a perilous journey of three hundred miles, through a wild and mountainous country, covered with snow, which in some places was fifty or sixty feet deep, and knowing that at any time they were likely to fall in with a savage grizzly, or the still more savage Indian. With a farewell cheer from their comrades, and with

> "Health that mocks the doctors' rules,
> And knowledge never learned in schools,"

they commenced their first day's journey to Fort Laramie. The first night they thought they had accomplished about twenty-five miles of their journey, and they camped near a small stream. They scooped a hole in the snow, and breaking off some pine bushes for a bed, they rolled themselves in their blankets and buffalo robes and slept soundly till morning. They found, however, that the travel of the day before had strained their insteps to such a degree that they could scarcely walk, and it was only after a great deal of rubbing were they again able to travel with their snow shoes.

The second day they did not make more than ten miles before their feet gave completely out. They had reached the banks of a small river, comparatively free from snow, and had seated themselves on a log to rest, when a couple of deer came trotting down on the other side of the stream. Rose immediately took his rifle from its pouch and shot one of them. Then gathering a lot of dry limbs, they built a fire and feasted sumptuously on venison steak.   Then replenishing their fires they laid down between it and the log and slept comfortably till morning, and finding their insteps were too sore to travel, they rested there another day. The next morning, being thoroughly rested, Rose proposed they should put some soft buffalo skin between the strap of the snow-shoe and instep. This they found acted like a charm, and from that time forward they had no more trouble with their snow-shoes.

After about two weeks travel they struck the Sweet Water, and a few days after reached the North Platte, and, to their great joy, landed at Fort Laramie two days before Christmas.

Here they found Tom Biggs and his company, who had arrived at the fort in safety, but owing to the winter having set in so early, they were afraid to attempt to rejoin their company.

Rose and his comrade, Woods, were hospitably received and entertained, and they were glad to get a few days rest after their long and perilous journey.

Christmas was celebrated at the fort in the usual manner.   A cannon that was mounted in the bastian was heavily loaded, to be shot off as a grand Christmas gun.   In order to make a louder report, an old pair of buckskin pants and several pairs of old moccasins were rammed in, till the gun was filled nearly to the muzzle. The gunner refused to touch off the cannon, as he said he was sure it would burst. Dave Crow, one of the trappers, and a particular friend of Rose's, took the iron rod from the fire and touched it off, and, as the gunner predicted, it flew into a hundred pieces. One of the splinter's broke Crow's leg. This was the man that waited on Rose so kindly when he received his wound from the Blackfeet.

One of the men at the fort pretended to know all about dressing the wound, and Rose left his friend in his care. Rose was compelled to go up the Chugwater with the horses, as the pasture was getting very poor round about the fort.

During his absence his friend Crow died, the man having bandaged his leg so tight that mortification set in.

The trappers had a jolly time at the fort during the winter. Rose says it was the most pleasant winter he spent during his stay in the mountains.

While Rose was at the fort, Massellino, who had been up at Chugwater, came in, bringing with him a vial containing about an ounce of gold dust. The trappers at first laughed at the idea of its being gold; but the Mexican assured them that it was the pure stuff, and added that his father and himself had worked in a gold mine for years.

When the spring set it, Rose, together with Biggs' party, started to join Bridger's company, having with them about fifteen pack horses and mules loaded with goods and supplies. They journeyed about a week without meeting with any adventure worth relating, when one day about noon, having ascended a steep ridge, they came upon a band of about fifty Grovout Indians. These Indians are not as fierce or savage as the Blackfeet, but are very impudent and overbearing when they think they have the upper hand. The Grovouts halted about one hundred and fifty yards from the trappers, and the chief came forward to hold a pow-wow, and Biggs, being the leader of the party, went out to meet him. The chief assumed a very dictatorial tone. He said his band was poor and needed supplies, and that if the white men would give up the pack horses and mules, with their packs, he would allow the trappers to go on their way unmolested; if not, they must take the consequences. Biggs said he would return to his company and consult with his men.

This he did, looking pretty badly scared, and evidently showing the white feather. He told the trappers that he thought it was the best thing they could do, and that perhaps to give up their horses and goods would be the only chance to save their lives.

This speech made Rose very angry. He represented to Biggs and the trappers that himself and his comrade, Wood, had traveled three hundred miles in the depth of winter to secure the much-needed supplies for their company, and that the very existence of the American Fur Company depended on these supplies reaching them. He pointed out that the Grovouts were not much more than three to one; that they were poorly armed, not having more than a dozen fusees among them, the balance of their arms being bows and arrows and spears; that he would make peaceable terms with them if possible; but that he would fight as long as he had a bullet in his pouch before they should take a single horse or a pack.

Most of the trappers coincided with the views expressed by Rose, and the chief again came out, accompanied by a half-breed as interpreter, and Rose and Massillino were appointed to meet them and state the case. Rose told the chief that the white man had always been friendly to the Grovouts, and that they were willing to remain so, and would make him some handsome presents. He stated that they were well armed, and before they would give up a single horse or pack they would fight to the death. And not to be beaten in bombast, Rose informed the chief that they had often whipped bands of Blackfeet when the odds were much greater against them.

This speech acted like magic, and the chief and his interpreter returned to his band quite crest-fallen. Rose and his party then took the packs from the mules, and the barrels of fifteen rifles were pointed at the Indians, who, seeing the white men determined, accepted of a few butcher knives and a couple of red blankets, and the trappers went on their way rejoicing.

In a few days they arrived on the Rosebud, where they met with Bridger and his company, and the delight on receiving the long looked for supplies can better be imagined than described.

CHAPTER XXX.

IN WHICH THE CAMP IS ATTACKED BY A MAD WOLF.
THE RENDEZVOUS—ROSE IS PERSUADED TO RETURN
TO ST. LOUIS—A HUNTING ADVENTURE.

As soon as Bridger's company had received the supplies they so much needed, they left the Rose-bud and started for the headwaters of Powder river. Here they commenced trapping on some of the small tributaries running into that stream; but it was evident there was a decided falling off of beaver. The streams had all been trapped over, both by the Hudson Bay and Rocky Mountain Fur Companies, and it was evident that unless some better location could be found their catch that spring would be very light.

One beautiful night, in the month of May, the trappers had reached a small stream, and not having had time to put up their lodges, they, as usual, camped for the night, placing one of the trappers, by the name of Nicholas Gann, on guard. It was a bright moonlight night, and Gann perceived a large timber-wolf rushing toward the camp, foaming at the mouth, and showing evident signs of being in a rabid condition. Gann shot at the animal, but unfortunately missed it, and the wolf darted into the camp, running over the bodies of the sleeping trappers, and biting and snapping at everything that came in his way. First one trapper would put his head out from under his buffalo robe and call out, "Here it is, Gann!" Then half a dozen trappers would call out simultaneously, "Here it is, Gann!" This expression was taken up by the whole crowd, and "Here it is, Gann!" resounded on all sides, amid shouts of laughter. But the mad wolf proved to be no laughing matter. The rabid animal had bitten several of the horses, and the trappers were afraid to shoot for fear of killing some of the animals. At length one of the men knocked the wolf on the head with the butt of his musket. The next morning it was discovered that two of the men had been severely bitten; they were named respectively Sloat and Scott, and they were badly scared when they found the wolf had been mad, and insisted on starting immediately for Fort Laramie to obtain for themselves surgical aid. We may here state that Sloat was never heard of again. Scott was found dead on a bluff about forty miles from Fort Laramie. He was identified by his rifle and shot-bag. The trappers were obliged to kill the animals that were bitten, as they were all attacked by hydrophobia a short time after.

As soon as the spring trapping was over the men repaired to the usual place of rendezvous, and as the caravan from St. Louis had not yet arrived, Rose, in company with about a dozen of the other trappers, started out to meet it. On the third day they fell in with the St. Louis train, and Rose was delighted to find that Captain Stewart and Logan Fontanelle accompanied the train. The latter named young man was the son of the St. Louis partner of the Fur Company. He had become acquainted with Rose on a former visit to the mountains, and they had always been excellent friends. Rose was also much pleased to renew his acquaintance with Captain Stewart.

The usual amount of fun and frolic was indulged in at the rendezvous, Captain Stewart giving the trappers several big treats and making them some valuable presents.

As Fontanelle was a young man of excellent education, Rose got him to write a letter to Pennsylvania to his friends, he being no penman himself, and consequently had not written since his stay in the mountains. In his letter he informed his relatives that he had received a bad wound in his arm which would be apt to cripple him for life, and that, as he had no education, he did not think it would be good policy to return home, as he could not now make a living at hard work. This letter was given to Captain Stewart, who took it with him on his return to St. Louis, and mailed it to his friends.

A few days after this, Fontanelle and Rose having walked out together, the young man endeavored to persuade Rose to return with him to the States. He said if Rose would go back and attend school for a few months, so as to be able to read and write correctly, he would get him a good situation in the Fur Company that would enable him to make a living without working too hard. To this Rose at length agreed, and he commenced at once making preparations to return with the caravan to St. Louis when the rendezvous was over. He accordingly went to Captain Stewart and told him not to send the letter, but the Captain informed him that the letter would beat him home.

About a week before the caravan started Captain Stewart, Fontanelle, Rose, Kit Carson, and three or four of the other trappers started on a big hunt, intending it to be the last before they left the mountains. Captain Stewart had furnished some of his best horses for the trip. About ten miles from camp, the hunters reached an extended plain, and were much pleased to discover a small herd of buffalo, not more than two miles distant. It was a beautiful, calm day. Not a breath of wind seemed to be stirring, and a halt was at once called.

Rose and Cason, who were the most experienced hunters, rode a little in advance. Then each man placed his fore finger in his mouth, holding it there for some little time, then raised it above his head, and by this means discovered from which quarter what little wind there was, was coming. The air appeared to come from the south, and the hunters immediately began circling around, so as to approach the buffalo from the north, and thereby prevent the animals from scenting them. By this means they contrived to get within a quarter of a mile of the herd before they began to stampede.

As soon as the buffalo began to get restless, the hunters put spurs to their horses, and started at full speed for the herd, each man selecting his intended victim. Rose gave chase to a young heifer, but the animal ran like a deer, and although he was well mounted, they ran nearly a mile before he came up with it. As he was about to ride up, rifle in hand, he saw before him a small gully about eight feet wide. Over this the heifer sprang lightly and darted away. Not so with the horse. On reaching the edge of the gully he came to a dead stop. Now, although the horse came to a sudden stand-still, Rose did not, but flew over the animal's head and struck the opposite side of the gully with such force that he lay for some seconds, serenely contemplating one or two thousand stars that seemer to be shooting helter-skelter, hither and thither, across his mental vision. Quickly recovering, however, he sprang to his feet, gave half a dozen heavy gasps, and stretching himself to see that no bones were broken, he led his horse over the gully, remounted, and again started in pursuit of the buffalo, now about half a mile distant.

After a race of about two miles, he once more came up with the heifer; but upon pointing his rifle, discovered, to his great amazement, that his fall had bent the weapon into the shape of a bow, and as a shooting-iron it was useless.

On returning, he was heartily laughed at by his companions, who had succeeded in killing three of the buffalo. The animals were soon skinned, and the meat packed, and the hunters started for a rocky ravine about two miles distant, up which it was almost impossible for the horses to travel. Just as they were considering what was best to be done, Rose, who was a little in advance, called out: "There's 'Caleb!'" and sure enough, not more than three hundred yards distant was a large grizzly bear climbing over the rocks and ascending the ravine. He had evidently seen them, as he seemed in a great hurry to get away. The men immediately dismounted and started in pursuit, leaving the horses in the care of Bill Doty, one of the trappers. After two hours' scrambling over the rocks, Kit Carson, who was in advance, succeeded in wounding the bear, who immediately turned at bay and came rushing toward them. Captain Stewart, who was standing on a rock, waited till the bear came within ten yards of him, the other trappers wishing to give him a chance to distinguish himself. The Captain shot the bear, slightly wounding it. This only made the animal more savage, and he at once made a dash at the Captain, who would most certainly have fared badly had not Rose, who was expecting something of this sort, shot the bear through the lungs, killing him instantly.

"Caleb" was soon skinned, and the men again descended the ravine. At the lower end they were met by Bill Williams, (this is the man who afterwards led Fremont into so much trouble,) who, with a very deplorable countenance, informed them that a band of Crows had stolen all the horses but two, these having strayed behind some rocks, had not been seen by the Indians. On finding the route the Crows had taken led toward the rendezvous, they immediately started in that direction to get fresh horses and reinforcements, while Carson and Rose, mounting the horses, followed the Indian trail. As soon as they reached the rendezvous, twenty trappers mounted and immediately joined Stewart in the pursuit. They soon found the trail and galloped on till night, when they halted with the intention of renewing the chase the next day. About midnight they were joined by Rose and Carson, who informed them that the Crows had camped not more than six miles distant. On hearing this the trappers again mounted, and led by Carson and Williams, Rose remaining behind, not wishing to be recognized by his old enemies,

the Crows, soon came in sight of the Crow camp.
Here they halted till daylight. They then rode
forward till within one hundred yards of the Indian
band. Carson then went forward and signified
they wanted to hold a "pow-wow." Two of their
chiefs came out to meet them, and Carson at once
asked why they had stolen their horses. The chief
said that in all his dealings with the white men
his people had always been cheated; that the white
men had stolen their horses, killed their warriors,
and made widows in their villages, and that in
stealing the horses he had done no worse to the
white man than the white man had done to him.
Carson, who was best posted in Indian talk, told
the chief that the white men had always done what
they had agreed to do with the Indians, and the
Indians always appeared quite satisfied; but the
Crows had stolen five horses from the white men
for every one the white men had stolen from them;
that their warriors had never been slain unless in
self defense, or when they were caught stealing
around the camp; that they were willing to make
the Crows some presents, and that if the horses
were not handed over at once there would be more
widows to lament before they were an hour older.
The chiefs consulted together for some time, and
at length agreed to give up the horses. Captain

Stewart making them a present of half a dozen blankets and a couple of fusees, and the trappers returned once more to the rendezvous rejoiced at their success.

This was Rose's last adventure before starting for St. Louis.

CHAPTER XXXI.

IN WHICH ROSE STARTS FOR ST. LOUIS—GRAND RE-
CEPTION AT WESTPORT—ARRIVES AT ST. LOUIS.

At length the time arrived for the St. Louis train to start, and Rose felt very sad at shaking hands for the last time with his old comrades. He thought of the many happy days he had spent in their company, and the thrilling adventures they had had together. But sentimentality is not one of the characteristics of the Rocky Mountain trapper. With proverbial recklessness, he soon threw off the feeling of care and depression caused by the parting, and in less than an hour was laughing and chatting with Captain Stewart as merrily as if nothing of the kind had occurred.

Captain Stewart's principal object in accompanying the St. Louis caravan was to have a grand hunt in crossing the plains to and from the Rocky Mountains, and he generally contrived, in company with some of the other trappers, to take a two weeks' hunt through the mountains while the rendezvous lasted, and always took back with him to the States the skins of the animals that were slain. These he eventually took back with him to England, as trophies of his wonderful hunting excursions in the western wilds of America.

Captain Stewart, Rose and Fontanelle generally rode in advance of the train. They, with one or two of the other trappers, supplying the company with meat, and, with the exception of some hunting adventures, nothing worthy of interest occurred, and the train reached Fort Laramie in safety. Here they halted a couple of days. Captain Stewart had brought a cart with him from St. Louis, which he had left at the fort on his outward trip, not being able to take it any farther west. This was filled with the heavy packs of buffalo and grizzly skins, and was placed under the care of Ward, who the reader knows as "Figurehead," who was also bound for St. Louis. On the third day after their arrival at Fort Laramie the train started and continued unmolested in its course till they reached the Blue, when Captain Stewart sent an express forward to Westport with the intention of having a grand entertainment prepared on their arrival at that place; and when Rose and his com-

panions arrived they found a grand treat awaiting
them.   At the Captain's request they ate their
repast the same as if they had been in the mountains, trapper fashion, using only their hunting
knives and their fingers.   A large crowd of people
were there to see the performance, and they were
astonished to see how rapidly and dextrously a
turkey would be dissected, and divided up, each
man gnawing away at his piece.   While staying in
Westport, the packs had been stowed away in a log
warehouse, about three miles from town, at the
mouth of the Kaw, or what is now called the
Kansas river.   Here Rose placed his possible sack.
This being a large leather sack that would hold
about three bushels.   In this bag Rose had placed
all the curiosities he had collected during his stay
in the mountains, among which was a petrified
wolf's head, and a petrified snake nearly three feet
long.   He had also a splendid Indian bow, covered
with snake skin, and a beautiful quiver, containing
about fifty arrows.   He had also several pairs of
beautifully worked moccasins and leggins, presented to him by the Crows during his captivity.
Two pairs of these had been worked by Chilsipee,
during her stay with the trappers.   In fact, the
bag was filled with curiosities of every description,
and Rose valued it more than all the money he

had earned during his stay in the mountains, and during their stay in Westport "Figurehead" was left in charge of the warehouse.

Rose and his companions had a good time in Westport for several days, and were delighted to enjoy once more the luxuries of civilized life. Rose had neither shaved or cut his hair during his stay in the mountains, and the Westport barber informed him if he did not shave and have his hair trimmed, he would have half the boys in St. Louis running after him. Rose accordingly allowed the barber to operate on him, and after exchanging his buckskin suit for a more fashionable one he strode forth looking once more like a civilized human being. On the arrival of the steamboat, Rose started for the warehouse to look out for his possible sack, but, to his great mortification, found that "Figurehead" had taken it, and started three days before in a canoe, but whether across or down the river, no one could inform him, and that was the last he ever heard of "Figurehead" or his bag of curiosities. He was very much provoked and put out by the loss; but as he was not one to "cry over spilt milk," he soon regained his accustomed serenity.

The boat being now ready for the return trip, our trappers went on board and had a very pleasant voyage down the Missouri, and landed safely in St. Louis in the beginning of October.

Logan Fontanelle at once took Rose to a private boarding house, kept by a widow lady by the name of Davis, and here Rose found himself in very comfortable quarters.

The markets and stores of St. Louis were filled with fruits of every description, and, as Rose had neither seen or tasted anything of the kind during his stay in the mountains, he pitched in a little too heavy, and as a natural consequence he became very unwell and had to send for the doctor.

His complaint proved to be chills and fever, and he was confined to his bed for two weeks. When he was once more able to sit up he asked the doctor who boarded in the same house with him, the amount of his bill. The doctor said as he had had a hard way of making his money, trapping in the mountains, and as he (the doctor) had but very little way to travel (being in the same house) he would make the bill as light as possible. That, in fact, he would only charge him three dollars a visit, and as he had some times visited him three times a day the bill assumed rather large proportions for a two weeks' sickness.

When Rose was once more able to come down stairs he was seated in the parlor one morning when some one entered the room, and Rose was both delighted and astonished to see standing before him his old friend and companion, Joe Lewis.

Joe was much pleased to meet his old friend once again, and gave him a full account of his adventures after escaping from the Indians, and his fearful trials and difficulties in crossing the plains to Fort Laramie, being without food or a rifle to procure it, and reached the fort in a deplorable condition. From thence he went with a train to St. Louis. Here, after some time, he was engaged by a surveying party, and had continued with them, surveying in the neighborhood of St. Paul, Minnesota, and had only returned to St. Louis about two weeks before, and, on making some inquiries at the headquarters of the Fur Company, had ascertained that Rose had returned to St. Louis, and he at once hunted him up.

After the friends had deliberated for some time, they both felt a strong inclination to visit once more their home and friends.

Joe Lewis had an excellent situation in the surveying company, and Rose had been promised an easy position by his friend, Logan Fontanelle, and had intended at once to commence acquiring an education, but the two friends meeting together knocked all their plans on the head, and the more they talked about home the more homesick they became, and they made up their minds to start down the river on the first boat, on their return trip to New Castle.

CHAPTER XXXII.

IN WHICH ROSE AND HIS FRIEND LEWIS RETURN HOME. GRAND RECEPTION—HE BECOMES A SCHOOL TEACHER—CONCLUDING REMARKS.

After taking leave of his kind hostess, Mrs. Davis, and her daughter, who had attended on him during his sickness as kindly and tenderly as if he had been one of the family, he, in company with Joe Lewis and Logan Fontanelle, started for the steamboat landing. On their way thither Logan continued to impress on the mind of Rose the necessity of at once acquiring an education, so that he might be qualified to fill a position that would enable him to gain a livelihood without resorting to hard work, for which, on account of his wounded arm, he was now totally unfitted. Bidding Logan farewell, our two young travelers boarded a boat bound for Pittsburg, and were soon steaming down the Mississippi.

They had a very pleasant voyage, in which nothing worth narrating occurred, and in due time were landed at Beaver Point, and the young men were delighted as they once more caught sight of the old familiar landmarks, and they now felt that really and truly they were nearing home.

One of the first persons they met after landing was their old friend, Joseph T. Boyd, and from him they received the first news from home. He informed them that not a death had occurred in either of their families during their absence, and that they were all in good health.

After dinner they boarded the New Castle packet, commanded by Captain Stone, who was afterwards landlord of the Cochran House.

In some way Mr. Joseph T. Boyd had contrived to send an express to New Castle, informing them of the wanderers return, and on reaching Moravia they were met by Thomas Lewis, the brother of Joe, who was delighted at once more meeting them. It was night when they reached the guard-lock, and they saw that the American House, kept by Andy Lewis, the father of Joe, was brilliantly illuminated, and many of their friends were at the lock to welcome them home. At the American House, they found that Joe's sisters, Eleanor and Elvira, had not been idle, and that a grand entertainment had been prepared for them; that Andy, the father, had "killed the fatted calf," and that everything betokened a hearty and a loving welcome home. Among the old friends who were there to welcome them was Dr. Shaw, in whose family Rose had once resided, Judge Reynolds, Johnnie Wilson, and many others. In fact, the bar-room and parlor were filled with old friends, all anxious to shake hands with and get a sight of the Rocky Mountain trappers.

Rose could not get away from the crowd till after midnight, when he was escorted by several friends to the residence of his parents, in Croton, who were rejoiced at once more beholding their long lost son.

Rose found on his return home that his parents were in rather straightened circumstances, and that the house in which they resided was a very poor one, and he at once bought a piece of property and put up a comfortable dwelling, near where the residence of Paul Butz now stands.

One of the first things Rose did after resting a few days was to purchase some school books. These consisted of a spelling book, English reader, Murray's grammar and the Western calculator. These school books had been in use nearly forty years, children studying in the same books their parents had used before them.

Rose, to use his own expression, "soon fell in love with his school books," and studied energetically night and day, and in November '38 he entered a school taught by Chas. Bligh. In three months, by diligence and hard study, he could read tolerably well, write a good, plain copy and had mastered the Western calculator as far as cube root, and had made considerable advance in grammar and rhetoric. He also become an adept at mending and making pens, and often assisted the teacher in this now obsolete work.

In February, at the urgent request of both pupils and parents, he took charge of the same school. This may appear to my readers a bold undertaking, but Rose, with his indomitable energy, resolved not to stick. He would often sit up and study to the "wee sma' hours" in order to qualify himself for the next day's studies, some of his pupils being as far advanced as himself. This school he continued to teach for two or three years.

In '39 he became acquainted with Dr. Charles T. Whippo, who, on discovering his anxiety to acquire an education, and observing how diligently he worked for that purpose, was much pleased with him and assisted him in many ways.

Dr. Whippo, as many of our readers will remember, was a scholar and a gentleman, and was at this time president of the board of trustees of the female seminary in New Castle. A gentleman named Hewitt was the teacher, and Dr. Whippo made arrangements with him to hear Rose recite in the evening at his private residence, and he also frequently pointed out to him the great advantage of acquiring a good education, and stimulated his endeavors by commending highly the progress he had already made.

Among Rose's classmates with Mr. Hewitt was John McGuffin, Lafayette Ketler, and Alexander Long, of Cincinnati, who has since figured largely in the politics of Ohio. He was spending the summer with his parents, Arthur G., and Aunt Katy Long.

Rose was now in a fair way to prosperity. His parents were comfortably settled in their new home; he had purchased twelve acres of land in Croton from Dr. Whippo. This land he laid off into lots and sold them to good advantage. He had gained the respect and esteem of both pupils and parents, and already had the credit of being an excellent teacher, and a rising young man. He continued to study and teach summer and winter for about twelve years, and taught every winter since, and has never lost an hour from school on account of sickness. His teachings have all been in what is now Lawrence county. He has taught in all the wards of New Castle, in Neshannock, Hickory, Slipperyrock, Big Beaver, Taylor and Shenango townships: the most in the latter. And he says he feels prouder of his record to-day as a teacher, and his pupils, than he did of gaining the trappers' prize. Many of his pupils fill prominent and responsible positions. Some are settled in the very scenes of his adventures in the Rockies; in Colorado, Utah, Wyoming, Idaho, California and Montana. Many fell on the battle fields and others starved in those miserable prison pens of the South.

Among his pupils in New Castle, Pa., were:

His Honor, Mayor McChesney,

Capt. Wm. H. McCandless and wife,

Geo. V. Boyles and wife,

Sylvester Gaston and wife,

Cowden Bleakley and wife,

Dr. J. K. Pollock,

The Stritmater Brothers,

The Pearson Brothers,

The Hill Brothers,

John Potter,

Samuel Nicklin,

James McConahy, the jeweler and optician,

Andrew Hutton,

Dr. H. R. Harbison, dentist,

Dr. S. E. McCreary, and many others.

Following is a list of Mr. Rose's pupils that have been, and are, employed as teachers in our public schools, and all in Lawrence county except two.

Thomas McCreary, deceased,

Martha E. McCreary, now Mrs. Captain Moffet, teaching No. 8, New Castle, Pa.,

Lizzie McCreary, Neshannock tp., Lawrence Co., Pa.,

R. V. Thompson, teaching in Neshannock tp., Lawrence county, Pa.

R. S. Brackenridge, teaching in Cattaraugus county, N. Y.

Sara Gibson, now Mrs. Russel,———, Ill.

Rebecca Lutton, now Mrs. Trimble,———, Ill.

S. J. Kerr, now Mrs. Rigby, Youngstown, O.

John McKee, physician, Princeton, Lawrence county, Pa.

J. I. McKee, physician, Washington county, Pa.

Jennie McKee, now Mrs. Dr. D. P. Jackson, Lebanon, N. J.

Anna M. McKee, now Mrs. Rev. McKinley, Barnet, Caledonia county, Vt.

Bella McKee, teaching in Mahoningtown schools, Lawrence county, Pa.

J. S. DuShane, teaching West New Castle schools, Lawrence county, Pa.

Della McMillen, now Mrs. J. S. DuShane, teaching Lincoln schools, New Castle, Pa.

G. W. Leslie, Slipperyrock tp., Lawrence county, Pa.

C. M. Hege, New Castle, Pa.

Amanda C. Hege, now Mrs. Ferguson, Wayne tp., Lawrence county, Pa.

Mary J. Rose, now Mrs. H. H. Warnock, Shenango tp., Lawrence county, Pa.

James V. Rose, Sharon, Mercer county, Pa.

George Rose, Shawneetown, Illinois.

C. H. Akens, student of law, New Castle, Pa.

Sarah Akens, since Mrs. Jos. M. Wilkison, dec'd.

Jos. Akens, New Castle, Pa.

Lafayette Baldwin, Shenango tp., Lawrence county, Pa.

S. R. Baldwin, teaching in Shenango tp., Lawrence county, Pa.

A. B. White, New Castle, Lawrence county, Pa.

Lizzie Kulen, now Mrs. S. Gibson, Shenango tp., Lawrence county, Pa.

Samuel Gibson, Shenango tp., Lawrence county, Pa.

Amanda Hazen, Shenango tp., dec'd.

Frances Leslie, New Castle, Pa.

J. F. Mayne, teaching in Shenango tp., Lawrence county, Pa.

Jennie Hill, now Mrs. Prince, Summers county, W. Va.

Sarah Miller, now Mrs. S. G. Alford, Slipperyrock tp., Lawrence county, Pa.

Will J. Irvin, dec'd.

Mary Irvin, dec'd.

Agnes Irvin, teaching in Wampum, Lawrence county, Pa.

Ray Irvin, teaching in Big Beaver tp., Lawrence county, Pa.

Tillie Whan, teaching in New Castle schools.

Maggie Whan, Big Beaver tp., Lawrence county, Pa.

D. P. Jackson, now Dr. Jackson, Lebanon, N. J.

Mollie Miller, now Mrs. Wymer, Shenango tp., Lawrence county, Pa.

Dora Aiken, now Mrs. Vanhorn, Slipperyrock tp., Lawrence county, Pa.

Mary Lanham, now Mrs. John T. Phillips, New Castle, Pa.

Mary McMillen, now Mrs. G. L. Leslie, warden of City Home, New Castle, Pa.

Alexander Aiken, now Rev. Aiken, York county, Pa.

V. M. Brown, teaching in Taylor tp., Lawrence county, Pa.

Scott D. Long, now attorney-at-law, New Castle, Pa.

James Sherrard, Shenango, Lawrence county, Pa.

J. H. Lutton, teaching in Indian Territory.

Leander Lutton, New Castle, Pa.

Charles Nash, now attorney-at-law, St. Paul, Minn.

Ed. Jackson, now Hon. Ed. Jackson, attorney-at-law, Mercer, Pa.

Hugh Gibson, deceased.

Rebecca Alford, deceased.

Sarah A. Gaston, deceased.

Tillie Aiken, now Mrs. Forbes, Scott tp., Lawrence county, Pa.

Rosa H. Frew, teaching in Slipperyrock tp., Lawrence county, Pa.

Albert W. Harbison, proprietor and manager of Clinton coal mines.

Sylvester Gaston, New Castle, Pa.

Maggie Harbison, Shenango township, Lawrence county, Pa.

Zebina Allen, Shenango township, Lawrence county, Pa.

Norman Reed, Shenango township, Lawrence county, Pa.

G. L. Reno, teaching in Shenango township, Lawrence county, Pa.

Mr. Rose served in Neshannock township as school director for a number of years, and was appointed by the board to examine candidates or applicants for schools. In '49 he was elected County Auditor for three years, and in '51 he moved into Shenango township and filled the same position in the School Board that he had in Neshannock. He was an acting justice of the peace for fifteen years in Shenango township.

Mr. Rose has for many years been an earnest and consistent worker in the church, and during the last forty-five years he has filled a place in the Sabbath School, either as superintendent or teacher.

We are now about to bring our sketch of his adventures to an end; but we beg leave to state that his history is not yet complete. He is still a hale, hearty, energetic man, and we hope may have many years of life and usefulness before him; and in bidding our readers farewell, we conclude our share of the adventures of Isaac P. Rose.

APPENDIX.

MASSACRE OF DR. WHITMAN, HIS WIFE AND
FAMILY, AT WAIILATPU, BY THE INDIANS,
NOV. 29, 1847.

Early in the spring of '48, Mr. Isaac P. Rose was
very much shocked to hear that Dr. Whitman, his
wife and family, had been murdered by the Indians.
Mr. Rose was well acquainted with the Doctor and
his lady, having, as our readers are aware, camped
with them some length of time in the Rocky
Mountains. He was very anxious to get the par-
ticulars of the horrid event, and succeeded after
some little time, in getting the full details of the
bloody tragedy, and these we are about to lay
before our readers. It appears, as far back as '42,
the Indians began to be very much dissatisfied,
and perhaps not without a cause. Emigrants were
continually arriving across the mountains and set-
tling in the Willamette valley. Here they built
houses fenced in land, cut down timber, and killed
game and the Indians discovered that unless

something was done, the land would soon be appropriated by the white men, and the game driven off or destroyed.

The Cayutes and Nez Perces complained to the missionaries and fur traders time after time. They were informed by both these parties that the United States was going to send them blankets, guns, ammunition, etc., in exchange for the land. But as year after year went on, and none of these promises were ever fulfilled, the Indians became more and more dissatified, and an open rupture was anticipated by many of the settlers.

Another circumstance added much to the bad feeling of the Indians. Catholic missionaries had been for some years among them, and as soon as they got a foot-hold they endeavored to instil in the minds of these savage people that Dr. Whitman, and other missionaries of that class were not teaching them the true doctrine of salvation. The Presbyterians, on the other hand, were continually endeavoring to point out the errors and inconsistencies of the Roman Catholic Church, and the Indians soon began to be very much perplexed. They wondered how any set of men who worshipped the same God, and were trying to get to the same heaven, could possibly differ so much in opinion, and many of them began to think that both parties were mistaken, and that the whole thing was a humbug.

As their belief in Christianity began to weaken, their former savage nature began to assert its sway, and the Indians threatened that unless something was done they would take the matter into their own hands. They seemed to be more embittered against Dr. Whitman and his family than any one else. This was principally owing to his being one of the first missionaries, and consequently, more was expected from him than from any of the rest. Another reason was, that the forms and ceremonies of the Catholic religion appeared to take better with the Indians than the dry, theological and controversial doctrines preached by the Presbyterians. The former appealed to their senses, the latter to their reason, and as their senses were far more susceptible than their reasoning powers, the Catholics had the best of it; and this was one reason why they began to look on Dr. Whitman with suspicion and dislike.

There were so many causes at work to produce a revolution among the Indians, that it would be unfair to name any one as *the* cause. The last and immediate provocation was a season of severe sickness among them. The disease was measles, and was brought in the train of the immigration. This fact alone was enough to provoke the worst passions of the savage. The immigration in itself was a sufficient offense; the introduction, through them, of a pestilence, a still weightier one. It did not signify that Dr. Whitman had exerted himself night and day to give them relief. Their peculiar notions about a medicine-man made it the Doctor's duty to cure the sick; or made it the duty of the relatives of the dead and dying to avenge their deaths.

About this time a half-breed, by the name of Lewis, came to the mission with a company of emigrants, and concluded, as the season was late, to stay there through the winter. Dr. Whitman did not approve of this, as he was afraid their provisions would run short; but not liking to turn them out, he took several of them, together with the half-breed, into his employ. Lewis was a great rascal, and did all in his power to incite the Indians to open rebellion. He would repeat to them imaginary conversations he pretended to have heard between Dr. Whitman and his friends, in all of which the Indians were to be either killed or driven from their land, and when the measles was at its height, and the Indians were dying at the rate of four or five a day, Lewis repeated a conversation he pretended to have heard, in which Dr. Whitman told his wife that from that time forward, he intended to poison all the sick. The next patients the Doctor attended to were watched by the Indians with great earnestness, and unfortunately the next four or five, to whom he gave the medicine, died. This brought things to a crisis, and it was resolved among the Indians, that not only Dr. Whitman and his wife must die, but all the Americans at the mission.

On the 22d of November, Mr. Spalding arrived at the mission in company with his daughter, bringing with him several horse loads of grain to help feed the emigrants, being fearful they might run short. Dr. Whitman's family consisted of himself and wife, a young man named Rodgers, who was employed as a teacher, and also studying for the ministry, two young people, a brother and sister, named Bulee, seven orphan children of one family, whose parents had died on the road to Oregon in a previous year, named Sager, Helen Mar, the daughter of Joe Meek, another little half-breed girl, daughter of Bridger, the fur trader, a half-breed Spanish boy, whom the Doctor had brought up from infancy, and two sons of a Mr. Mansor, of the Hudson Bay Company. Besides these, there was half a dozen other families at the mission, and at the saw mill, twenty miles distant, five families more, in all, forty-six persons at Waiilatpu, and fifteen at the mill, who were among those who suffered by the attack. But there were also about the mission still others, —— Lewis, Nicholas Finlay and Joseph Stanfield, who probably knew what was about to take place, and may, therefore be reckoned among the conspirators.

While Mr. Spalding was at Waiilatpu, a message came from two Walla-Walla chiefs, living on the Umatilla river, to Dr. Whitman, desiring him to visit the sick in their village, and the two friends set out together to attend to the call on the evening of the 27th of November. The night was dark and the wind and rain beat furiously upon them, still the two gentlemen conversed freely on the dissatisfaction shown by the Indians, and the present gloomy outlook. They also spoke of the constant demands of the Indians to be paid for their wood, their water, their air, and their lands. Mr. Spalding spoke of the Catholic influence.

"We felt," he says, "that the present sickness afforded them a favorable opportunity to excite the Indians to drive us from the country, and all the movements about us seemed to indicate that this would soon be attempted, if not executed."

Dr. Whitman crossed the river, and after administering to the wants of the two chiefs, he took breakfast with the Catholic bishop, and recrossing the river, started for the mission about four o'clock in the afternoon, leaving Dr. Spalding to visit the sick and offer consolation to the dying in that neighborhood. Mr. Spalding discovered that all the Indians appeared to be laboring under a great secret. All the satisfaction he could get from Stickas, his Indian host, was that the Americans had been "decreed against" by his people.

Mr. Spalding did not feel uneasy, as he had often heard these threats before. At night he retired to his bed of skins, it being Monday evening, the 29th, but not to sleep, however, for on either side of him, an Indian woman sat down to chant the death-song, that frightful lament which announces danger and death. On being questioned, they would reveal nothing. On the following morning Mr. Spalding could no longer remain in uncertainty, but set out for Waiilatpu. As he mounted his horse to depart, an Indian woman placed her hand on the neck of his horse to arrest him, and pretending to be arranging his head-gear, said in a low voice to the rider, "Beware of the Cayutes of the mission." Now more than ever disturbed by this intimation that it was the mission which was threatened, he hurried forward, fearing for his daughter, and his friends. He proceeded without meeting any one until within sight of the Walla-Walla valley, almost in sight of the mission itself, when suddenly, at a wooded spot where the trail passes through a little hollow, he beheld two horsemen advancing, whom he watched with a fluttering heart; longing for and yet dreading, the news which the very air seemed whispering. The two horsemen proved to be the Catholic Vicar General, Bronillett, who, with a party of priests and nuns had arrived in that country only a few weeks previous, and their half-breed interpreter, both of whom were known to Mr. Spalding. They drew rein as they approached, Mr. Spalding anxiously inquiring:

"What news?"

"There are very many sick at the Whitman station," answered Bronillet, with evident embarrsssment.

"How are the Doctor and Mrs. Whitman?" asked Spalding anxiously.

"The Doctor is ill—is dead!" added the priest, reluctantly.

"And Mrs. Whitman?" gasped Spalding.

"Is dead also. The Indians have killed them."

"My daughter?" murmured the agonized questioner.

"Is safe with the other prisoners," answered Bronillet.

Mr. Spalding was horrified on hearing of the fearful tragedy that had been enacted at the mission, and knowing that his wife was in danger, that in fact, he was likely to be surrounded and murdered at any moment by the Cayutes, he gave his pack horse to Bronillet, and bidding that gentleman farewell, sought shelter in the woods till nightfall. During the night his horse got away from him, and Mr. Spalding was compelled to make the journey to Lapwai on foot, where he arrived in about ten days, nearly starved to death, his clothes torn to shreds and his feet fearfully lacerated by the cactus through which he was compelled to travel. On arriving at Lapwai, he was rejoiced to find that his wife and family had been preserved by the Nez Perces; but the fatigue and peril he had undergone, together with the horrible massacre of his friends, had such an effect on his norvous system, that it remained a wreck ever after.

Dr. Whitman did not reach the mission until twelve o'clock Sunday night, and although very tired with his long ride, he visited all the sick about the mission before retiring to rest, and early on Monday morning he again resumed his duties. It was noticed that during the day a great many Indians had gathered around the mission, but as they were butchering a beef, this was supposed to be the cause.

In the afternoon, Dr. Whitman came in, weary and dejected, and setting down in his chair, he took up his bible, as was his usual custom, and commenced to read. Mrs. Whitman had just gone into an adjoining room to attend to a Mrs. Osborne and her child, who were sick. Just about this time, several Indians came to the door and asked if they might come in, saying they wanted medicine. Dr. Whitman bade them enter, and, getting up, gave them what they wanted and again reseated himself. Scarcely had he done so, when Tam-a-has, an Indian, came up behind him, and struck him in the back of the head with a tomahawk. The first blow partly stunned him, and the Indian struck him a second time, and the Doctor fell lifeless to the floor. John Sager, who saw the act, sprang to his feet, and drawing a pistol, was about to fire on the assassin, when he, too, was knocked down, and cut and hacked in a fearful manner.

As soon as Mrs. Whitman heard what was going on, she stamped her feet in a frantic manner, and cried, "Oh, the Indians! the Indians!" and rushing into the room, with the assistance of her neighbors, she dragged her unconscious husband to a sofa, and laying him on it, she did all in her power to revive him; but he was too far gone to utter any intelligible word.

In the meantime the slaughter was going on outside, Tam-a-has and his party having left the apartment to join in it. And now the din became fearful. The roar of musketry, the yells of the Indians, and the screams and groans of the wounded and dying were listened to by the horror stricken inmates.

One of them told Mrs. Whitman that two of her friends were just being butchered beneath her window, and she rushed forward at once, as if her presence could save them. In front of the window stood the half-breed, Lewis, and she called out to him: "It is you, Lewis, who is doing this!" She had scarcely spoken, when a young Indian, who had been a great favorite at the mission, discharged his gun, the ball striking her in the right breast, and she fell without a groan. Quickly recovering, however, she contrived to crawl to the sofa, and knelt by the side of her husband.

Mr. Rodgers, and some of the female inmates of the mission now removed Mrs. Whitman to another apartment, and soon after the Indians came into the room where Dr. Whitman was lying, and commenced plundering the apartment, taking away everything they could carry off. One of them by the name of Te-lan-ka-itt, who had just joined the church of probation, cut and hacked the face of the still breathing missionary with his tomahawk, in a most shocking manner, rendering his features unrecognizable.

An Indian by the name of Tam-sak-y, called to Mrs. Whitman to come down into the sitting room. She told him she could not come as she was badly wounded. The Indians now said if she did not come down they would set fire to the house. She then, assisted by Mr. Rodgers, who was badly wounded, and had an arm broken, came into the room. As soon as the Indians saw her they fired a volley. Mr. Rodgers fell at once, mortally wounded, and Mrs. Whitman also received several wounds. She contrived, however, to reach the side of her husband, who had just breathed his last.

At two o'clock the massacre had commenced. It was now growing dusk, and the demons were eager to finish their work. Seeing that life still lingered in the mangled bodies of their victims, they finished their atrocities by hurling them into the mud and gore which filled the yard, and beating them upon their faces with whips and clubs, while the air was filled with the noise of their shouting, singing and dancing; the Indian women and children assisting at these orgies, as if the bible had never been preached to them. And thus, after eleven years of patient endeavor to save some heathen souls alive, perished Doctor and Mrs. Whitman.

One of the most extraordinary and thrilling adventures connected with this massacre, was the escape of Mr. Osborne and family.

After Dr. Whitman had been wounded, and the massacre had commenced, Mr. Osborne took his wife and three small children into their bedroom, adjoining their sitting room, and raising a plank, quickly thrust them into the space beneath, and then following, let the plank down to its place. Here they lay in mortal dread for several hours, listening to the tramp of many feet above them, and hearing with fright the yells of the savage Indians, and the screams and groans of the wounded and dying. They remained in their uncomfortable hiding place till darkness set in, and when all was quiet they left the mission and started for Walla-Walla.

They had scarcely traveled two miles, however, when Mrs. Osborne, who had just arisen from a bed of sickness, declared she could go no farther; and he was compelled to stop, secreting his family in some bushes. Here they remained, suffering with cold and insufficient food, having only a little bread and cold mush which they had found in the Doctor's house before leaving it. On Tuesday night, Mrs. O. was able to move about three miles more; and again they were compelled to stop. Mr. Osborne and his family were now in a desperate situation. They were benumbed with cold, and without food, and Mr. Osborne discovered that if something was not immediately done, they would certainly die of starvation.

Placing his wife and the two eldest children in the most sheltered situation he could find, he took the youngest one in his arms, and bidding them be of good cheer, as he would return as soon as possible with assistance, he left them with a heavy heart and started for Fort Walla-Walla, where he arrived before noon on Thursday.

Although Mr. McBean, who was a Catholic, received him with friendliness of manner, he refused him horses to go for Mrs. Osborne and his other children, and even refused to furnish food to relieve their hunger, telling him to go to the Umatilla, and forbidding his return to the fort. A little food was given to himself and child, who had been fasting since Monday night. Whether Mr. McBean would have allowed this man to perish, is uncertain; but certain it is, that some base or cowardly motive made him exceedingly cruel to Mr. Osborne and his family. While Mr. Osborne was partaking of his tea and crackers there arrived at the fort, Mr. Stanley, the artist, whom the reader will remember having met in the mountains several years before. When the case became known to him, he offered his horses immediately to go for Mrs. Orborne. Shamed into an appearance of humanity, McBean then furnished an Indian guide to accompany Mr. Osborne to the Umatilla, where he still insisted the fugitives should go, though this was in the murderer's country.

A little meat and a few crackers were furnished for the supper of the travelers; and with a handkerchief for his hatless head, and a pair of socks for his child's naked feet, (all furnished by Mr. Stanley,) Mr. Osborne set out to return to his suffering wife and children. He and his guide traveled rapidly, arriving in good time near the spot where he believed his family to be concealed. But the darkness had confused his recollections, and after beating the bushes till daylight, the unhappy husband and father was about to give up the search in despair, when his guide at length discovered their retreat.

The poor mother and children were barely alive, having suffered much from exposure and hunger, to say nothing of their fears. Mrs. Osborne was compelled to be tied to the Indian in order to sit on her horse. In this condition, the miserable fugitives turned toward the Umatilla, in obedience to the command of McBean, and were only saved from being murdered by a Cayute by the scornful words of their guide, who shamed the murderer from his purpose of slaughtering a sick and defenceless family.   At a Canadian farm house, where they stopped to change horses, they were but roughly received; and learning that Tam-sak-y's lodge was near by, Mrs. Osborne refused to proceed any farther toward the Umatilla.   She said, "I doubt if I can live to reach the Umatilla; and if I must die, I may as well die at the gates of the fort.   Let us then turn back to the fort."

To this the guide assented, saying it was not safe going among the Cayutes.   The little party, quite exhausted, reached Walla-Walla about ten o'clock at night, and were at once admitted.   Contrary to his former course, McBean now ordered a fire made to warm the benumbed travelers, who, after being made tolerably comfortable, were placed in a secret room of the fort.   Again Mr. Osborne was importuned to go away, down to the Umatilla, McBean promising to take care of his family, and furnish him with an outfit if he would do so.   Upon being asked to furnish a boat, and Indians to man it, in order that his family might accompany him, he replied that his Indians refused to go.

From all the reluctance, not only on the part of
McBean, but of the Indians also, to do any act
which appeared like befriending the Americans, it
would appear that there was a very general fear of
the Cayute Indians, and a belief that they were
about to inaugurate a general war upon the Americans, and their friends and allies. Mr. Osborne,
however, refused to leave his family behind, and
McBean was forced to let him remain until relief
came. When it did come at last, in the shape of
Mr. Ogden's party, Stickas, the chief who had
warned Mr. Spalding, showed his kind feeling for
the sufferers by removing his own cap and placing
it on Mr. Osborne's head, and by tying a handkerchief over the ears of Mrs. Osborne's little son, as
he said, "to keep him warm, going down the river."
Sadly, indeed, did the little ones who suffered by
the massacre at Waiilatpu, stand in need of any
christian kindness.

We thought it would be interesting to our
readers to give this short sketch of the sufferings
and fate of persons with whom Mr. Rose became
intimately acquainted while trapping in the Rocky
Mountains, and bidding farewell to our readers we
conclude the adventures of Isaac P. Rose.

THE LAST OF HIS TRIBE.

I am standing alone in the deep forest shade,
    And the wind whistles mournful and low;
I am roaming alone, where in childhood I played
With the friends of my youth, in the ever-green glade;
    My kindred! oh, where are they now?

The forest is green, as in days long ago,
    When my forefathers ruled here alone;
Nor thought of the misery, anguish and woe,
When they welcomed the pale-face, their deadliest foe,
    My kindred! oh, where are they gone?

A thousand brave warriors armed at my call,
    In their war paint and battle array;
Like pines of the forest: firm, stately and tall,
No hardships could tire them, no danger appall,
    My warriors! alas! where are they?

My wigwam that stood by the sycamore tree,
    'Neath the shade of its sheltering bough;
Oh! there I was happy, contented and free,
While blest with the love of my dark O-na-lee,
    My loved one, oh! where is she now?

The friends of my manhood and youth are no more;
    All gone are my warriors so brave—
In the arms she so loved, in deep sadness I bore,
My dark O-na-lee to the broad river shore,
    And laid her to rest in the grave!

I look for my wild native forest in vain,
    By the ax of the white man laid low;
In its place stand the fields of tall waving grain,
And their herd are now scattered o'er valley and plain,
    Where once roamed the wild buffalo.

"Back, red man, away to the west! to the west!
    Back! back!" is forever their cry,
Not a spot for the poor weary Indian to rest,
O'er all the broad lands that my fathers possessed—
    I'll away to the mountains to die.

To the blest hunting grounds of the red man I'll soar,
    When this sad, weary spirit is free;
There in peace and contentment to live as of yore,
And clasp to my fond, yearning bosom once more,
    My loved one, my dark O-na-lee.

FINIS

The Far Western Frontier

An Arno Press Collection

[Angel, Myron, editor]. **History of Nevada.** 1881.

Barnes, Demas. **From the Atlantic to the Pacific, Overland.** 1866.

Beadle, J[ohn] H[anson]. **The Undeveloped West; Or, Five Years in the Territories.** [1873].

Bidwell, John. **Echoes of the Past:** An Account of the First Emigrant Train to California. [1914].

Bowles, Samuel. **Our New West.** 1869.

Browne, J[ohn] Ross. **Adventures in the Apache Country.** 1871.

Browne, J[ohn] Ross. **Report of the Debates in the Convention of California, on the Formation of the State Constitution.** 1850.

Byers, W[illiam] N. and J[ohn] H. Kellom. **Hand Book to the Gold Fields of Nebraska and Kansas.** 1859.

Carvalho, S[olomon] N. **Incidents of Travel and Adventure in the Far West; with Col. Fremont's Last Expedition Across the Rocky Mountains.** 1857.

Clayton, William. **William Clayton's Journal.** 1921.

Cooke, P[hilip] St. G[eorge]. **Scenes and Adventures in the Army.** 1857.

Cornwallis, Kinahan. **The New El Dorado; Or, British Columbia.** 1858.

Davis, W[illiam] W. H. **El Gringo; Or, New Mexico and Her People.** 1857.

De Quille, Dan. (William Wright). **A History of the Comstock Silver Lode & Mines.** 1889.

Delano, A[lonzo]. **Life on the Plains and Among the Diggings;** Being Scenes and Adventures of an Overland Journey to California. 1854.

Ferguson, Charles D. **The Experiences of a Forty-niner in California.** (Originally published as *The Experiences of a Forty-niner During Thirty-four Years' Residence in California and Australia*). 1888.

Forbes, Alexander. **California:** A History of Upper and Lower California. 1839.

Fossett, Frank. **Colorado:** Its Gold and Silver Mines, Farms and Stock Ranges, and Health and Pleasure Resorts. 1879.

The Gold Mines of California: Two Guidebooks. 1973.

Gray, W[illiam] H[enry]. **A History of Oregon, 1792–1849.** 1870.

Green, Thomas J. **Journal of the Texian Expedition Against Mier.** 1845.

Henry, W[illiam] S[eaton]. **Campaign Sketches of the War with Mexico.** 1847.

[Hildreth, James]. **Dragoon Campaigns to the Rocky Mountains.** 1836.

Hines, Gustavus. **Oregon:** Its History, Condition and Prospects. 1851.

Holley, Mary Austin. **Texas:** Observations, Historical, Geographical and Descriptive. 1833.

Hollister, Ovando J[ames]. **The Mines of Colorado.** 1867.

Hughes, John T. **Doniphan's Expedition.** 1847.

Johnston, W[illiam] G. **Experiences of a Forty-niner.** 1892.

Jones, Anson. **Memoranda and Official Correspondence Relating to the Republic of Texas, Its History and Annexation.** 1859.

Kelly, William. **An Excursion to California Over the Prairie, Rocky Mountains, and Great Sierra Nevada.** 1851. 2 Volumes in 1.

Lee, D[aniel] and J[oseph] H. Frost. **Ten Years in Oregon.** 1844.

Macfie, Matthew. **Vancouver Island and British Columbia.** 1865.

Marsh, James B. **Four Years in the Rockies; Or, the Adventures of Isaac P. Rose.** 1884.

Mowry, Sylvester. **Arizona and Sonora:** The Geography, History, and Resources of the Silver Region of North America. 1864.

Mullan, John. **Miners and Travelers' Guide to Oregon, Washington, Idaho, Montana, Wyoming, and Colorado.** 1865.

Newell, C[hester]. **History of the Revolution in Texas.** 1838.

Parker, A[mos] A[ndrew]. **Trip to the West and Texas.** 1835.

Pattie, James O[hio]. **The Personal Narrative of James O. Pattie, of Kentucky.** 1831.

Rae, W[illiam] F[raser]. **Westward by Rail:** The New Route to the East. 1871.

Ryan, William Redmond. **Personal Adventures in Upper and Lower California, in 1848–9.** 1850/1851. 2 Volumes in 1.

Shaw, William. **Golden Dreams and Waking Realities:** Being the Adventures of a Gold-Seeker in California and the Pacific Islands. 1851.

Stuart, Granville. **Montana As It Is:** Being a General Description of its Resources. 1865.

Texas in 1840, Or the Emigrant's Guide to the New Republic. 1840.

Thornton, J. Quinn. **Oregon and California in 1848.** 1849. 2 Volumes in 1.

Upham, Samuel C. **Notes of a Voyage to California via Cape Horn, Together with Scenes in El Dorado, in the Years 1849–'50.** 1878.

Woods, Daniel B. **Sixteen Months at the Gold Diggings.** 1851.

Young, F[rank] G., editor. **The Correspondence and Journals of Captain Nathaniel J. Wyeth, 1831–6.** 1899.